The Puzzle of Me: Discovering the Why Behind Me

Shah Rukh

Published by Shah Rukh, 2024.

While every precaution has been taken in the preparation of this book, the publisher assumes no responsibility for errors or omissions, or for damages resulting from the use of the information contained herein.

THE PUZZLE OF ME: DISCOVERING THE WHY BEHIND ME

First edition. June 13, 2024.

Written by Shah Rukh.

Table of Contents

Prologue

In the intricate mosaic of life, each of us is a unique piece, shaped by the multitude of experiences, emotions, and choices that form our journey. "The Puzzle of Me: Discovering the Why Behind Me" is not just a collection of events and memories; it is a voyage into the depths of self-discovery, a quest to understand the intricate web of factors that make us who we are.

From the tender beginnings of childhood, where our identities first take root, to the turbulent waters of adolescence and the complex landscapes of adulthood, each chapter of our lives adds a new dimension to our personal puzzle. Along the way, we encounter joy and sorrow, triumphs and defeats, love and loss. These moments, whether fleeting or profound, leave indelible marks on our souls, shaping our character and influencing our paths.

This book is an exploration of those moments. It delves into the foundations laid by our families, the friendships that color our world, and the challenges that test our resilience. It examines how our environments, both physical and emotional, contribute to the development of our self-esteem, confidence, and overall sense of self.

As you turn these pages, you will journey through the phases of life, witnessing the evolution of a person navigating the complexities of existence. You will see how early experiences plant the seeds of our future selves, how the trials of adolescence forge our identity, and how the responsibilities and freedoms of adulthood refine our character.

But this is not just a story about growing up; it is an invitation to reflect on your own journey. It encourages you to consider the factors that have influenced who you are today and to appreciate the uniqueness of your own puzzle. Each chapter is a mirror, reflecting not just the life of the protagonist but also offering insights into your own experiences and growth.

In understanding the "why" behind ourselves, we find clarity and empowerment. We learn to embrace our strengths, acknowledge our weaknesses, and appreciate the intricate beauty of our individual journeys. "The Puzzle of Me" is a testament to the power of self-discovery and the ongoing adventure of becoming.

So, as you embark on this literary voyage, remember that each piece of your puzzle, no matter how small or seemingly insignificant, holds value. Together, they form the masterpiece of your life. Welcome to the journey of discovering the why behind you.

Chapter 1: The Beginning: A New Life

The beginning of life is a profound and intricate tapestry, woven with threads of countless experiences, influences, and emotions. At the heart of this tapestry lies the birth of an individual, a momentous event that marks the emergence of a unique consciousness into the world. This initial stage, often referred to as "The Beginning: A New Life," is not merely the commencement of physical existence but the start of an intricate journey that shapes the essence of who we become. From the very first breath, a newborn is immersed in a world that is both nurturing and challenging, setting the stage for the formation of personality, character, and identity.

From the moment of conception, the biological processes that culminate in birth begin to unfold, laying the foundation for physical, cognitive, and emotional development. The genetic blueprint inherited from parents plays a critical role in shaping various aspects of an individual, including physical attributes, temperament, and potential susceptibilities. However, it is important to recognize that this genetic inheritance is only one piece of the puzzle. The environment into which a child is born also plays a crucial role in shaping the course of their development. The dynamic interplay between genetics and environment begins even before birth, as the conditions within the womb can influence various aspects of development.

At birth, a newborn enters a world that is filled with sensory stimuli. The initial moments outside the womb are a profound sensory experience as the infant is exposed to light, sound, touch, and temperature in ways that were previously unfamiliar. These early experiences lay the groundwork for the development of the sensory and nervous systems, which are crucial for the perception and interaction with the world. The infant's early responses to these stimuli are often reflexive, but they gradually become more sophisticated as the brain and nervous system continue to develop.

One of the most significant influences in a newborn's life is the immediate family, particularly the parents or primary caregivers. The bond that forms between a parent and child is critical for the child's emotional and psychological development. This bond, often referred to as attachment, is a deep and enduring emotional connection that profoundly influences the child's sense of security and well-being. The quality of this attachment can have long-lasting effects on the individual's ability to form healthy relationships and cope with stress and adversity throughout life. Secure attachment, characterized by a caregiver's consistent responsiveness and nurturing, fosters a sense of trust and confidence in the child. Conversely, insecure attachment, which may result from neglect or inconsistent caregiving, can lead to difficulties in emotional regulation and relationship formation later in life.

As the infant grows, they begin to explore their surroundings, initially through simple actions such as grasping objects, making sounds, and eventually crawling and walking. These early explorations are crucial for cognitive development, as they allow the child to learn about cause and effect, spatial relationships, and the properties of objects. This period of exploration is also a time of significant brain development, with rapid growth and the formation of neural connections that will support more complex cognitive functions in the future.

The early years of life are also a time of significant emotional development. Infants and young children experience a wide range of emotions, from joy and excitement to fear and frustration. These emotions are often intense and can be expressed through behaviors such as crying, laughing, and tantrums. The way in which caregivers respond to these emotional expressions can have a profound impact on the child's emotional development. For example, a caregiver who provides comfort and support when a child is upset can help the child learn to regulate their emotions and develop a sense of emotional security. On the other hand, a caregiver who is dismissive or harsh may contribute to difficulties in emotional regulation and a sense of insecurity.

As the child continues to grow, they begin to develop a sense of self. This self-awareness emerges gradually and is influenced by a combination of biological, cognitive, and social factors. The child's interactions with caregivers and other significant figures play a crucial role in shaping their self-concept. Positive interactions, characterized by love, encouragement, and validation, help the child develop a sense of self-worth and confidence. Negative interactions, on the other hand, can contribute to feelings of inadequacy and low self-esteem. The development of self-awareness also involves the ability to recognize and understand one's own emotions, thoughts, and behaviors. This self-understanding is a key component of emotional intelligence and is critical for effective social interactions and relationships.

Throughout the early years of life, the child is also learning about the social world. This social learning occurs through interactions with caregivers, siblings, peers, and other individuals. The child observes and imitates the behaviors of others, learning about social norms, roles, and expectations. These early social experiences are crucial for the development of social skills and the ability to form and maintain relationships. The family, as the primary socializing agent, plays a central role in this process, providing the child with their first lessons in social behavior and values.

As the child reaches school age, they begin to interact with a broader social environment. The school setting introduces new social dynamics and expectations, as well as opportunities for learning and growth. The experiences and relationships formed during this period can have a lasting impact on the child's social development and sense of identity. Positive experiences in the school environment, such as supportive relationships with teachers and peers, can foster a sense of belonging and competence. Negative experiences, such as bullying or academic difficulties, can contribute to feelings of isolation and inadequacy.

The transition from childhood to adolescence marks a significant shift in the individual's developmental journey. Adolescence is a time of profound physical, cognitive, and emotional changes, as the individual undergoes puberty and begins to develop a more complex and nuanced understanding of themselves and the world. This period is often characterized by a search for identity, as the individual explores different aspects of themselves and seeks to define their place in the world. The experiences and relationships during this period can have a lasting impact on the individual's sense of self and their ability to navigate the challenges of adulthood.

Throughout this journey, the individual is constantly influenced by a complex interplay of factors, including biological predispositions, early experiences, family dynamics, social interactions, and cultural influences. Each of these factors contributes to the development of the individual's personality, character, and identity. The experiences and relationships that shape the early years of life lay the foundation for the individual's future development and the person they will become.

Chapter 2: First Steps: Exploring the World

The first steps of a child, metaphorically and literally, represent a monumental phase in human development that extends beyond physical movement. It is a period rich with exploration, discovery, and significant growth, marking the child's transition from a state of complete dependence to one of burgeoning autonomy. These early steps into the world set the stage for lifelong learning and development, laying the groundwork for the child's cognitive, emotional, and social capacities.

From the moment a child takes their first steps, they are embarking on a journey that involves not just mastering the mechanics of movement but also engaging with the world in profound and transformative ways. The act of walking, for instance, is a complex milestone that signifies the development of muscle strength, balance, and coordination. But more than that, it opens up a new realm of possibilities for exploration and interaction. Suddenly, the child is no longer confined to the immediate vicinity of where they were placed; they can move towards objects of interest, interact with their environment more directly, and experience the world from new perspectives. This newfound mobility is a crucial step in the development of autonomy and self-confidence, as the child learns to navigate their surroundings and achieve a degree of independence.

The exploration that begins with those first tentative steps is fueled by an innate curiosity and a desire to understand the world. This curiosity drives the child to investigate their environment, leading to a process of learning through discovery. As they move through different spaces, they encounter a variety of stimuli that challenge their senses and intellect. They touch objects to feel their textures, put things in their mouths to taste and understand them, listen to the different sounds around them, and observe the actions of others. Each of these experiences contributes to the child's growing knowledge and understanding of the world, helping to develop their cognitive abilities.

As the child explores their environment, they begin to develop a sense of spatial awareness. They learn to understand the relationships between different objects and spaces, gaining insights into concepts such as distance, direction, and size. This spatial understanding is fundamental to the development of problem-solving skills, as it allows the child to navigate around obstacles, retrieve objects, and engage in increasingly complex activities. The act of moving through space also enhances the child's proprioception, or the sense of the position and movement of their body parts, which is crucial for coordinated movement and physical competence.

The early exploration of the world also plays a vital role in the child's emotional development. As they move through different spaces and encounter new situations, they experience a range of emotions, from excitement and joy to frustration and fear. These emotional experiences are integral to the development of emotional intelligence, as they help the child learn to recognize, understand, and manage their feelings. For example, the joy of successfully reaching a desired object or destination can boost the child's confidence and self-esteem, while the frustration of being unable to overcome an obstacle can teach them about persistence and resilience. The child also begins to learn about empathy and social interaction through their encounters with others, as they observe and respond to the emotions and actions of those around them.

As the child's mobility and exploration skills improve, they become more adept at interacting with their environment in meaningful ways. This interaction is often facilitated by play, which is a fundamental aspect of early childhood development. Through play, children engage in activities that are both enjoyable and educational, allowing them to experiment with different roles, test their ideas, and develop their imagination. Play provides a safe and supportive context for children to explore their capabilities, try out new behaviors, and learn about the consequences of their actions. It also offers opportunities for social interaction, as children play with siblings, peers, and adults, learning about cooperation, sharing, and communication.

The social aspect of exploration is particularly significant, as it helps children to develop the skills they need to interact effectively with others. Through their interactions with caregivers, family members, and peers, children learn about social norms, values, and expectations. They observe the behaviors of others, imitate actions, and receive feedback on their own behaviors, which helps them to understand the dynamics of social relationships. These early social experiences are crucial for the development of social competence, as they teach children how to navigate the complexities of human interaction, build relationships, and resolve conflicts.

The process of exploration also contributes to the development of the child's identity. As they engage with the world and interact with others, they begin to form a sense of self. They learn about their own abilities, preferences, and characteristics, and start to understand how they are similar to or different from others. This growing self-awareness is a key aspect of identity development, as it helps children to define who they are and how they relate to the world around them. The experiences and feedback they receive during their early explorations can have a lasting impact on their self-concept and self-esteem, influencing their sense of competence and worth.

The role of caregivers in supporting and guiding the child's exploration is also crucial. Caregivers provide a safe and nurturing environment that encourages the child to explore and learn. They offer physical and emotional support, set appropriate boundaries, and provide opportunities for the child to engage in a variety of activities. They also serve as role models, demonstrating behaviors and attitudes that the child can emulate. The quality of the caregiving relationship can have a significant impact on the child's exploration and development, as it provides the foundation for the child's sense of security and confidence.

As the child continues to explore their environment, they encounter increasingly complex challenges and opportunities for learning. They begin to engage in more structured activities, such as puzzles, building blocks, and art projects, which help to develop their fine motor skills, problem-solving abilities, and creativity. They also start to participate in more organized social activities, such as group play, sports, and educational programs, which provide opportunities for further social interaction and learning. These activities help to expand the child's knowledge and skills, preparing them for the demands of school and the broader social world.

The transition from early childhood to school age represents a significant shift in the child's exploration and learning. The school environment introduces new challenges and opportunities, as the child is exposed to a wider range of experiences, subjects, and social interactions. The structured nature of the school setting provides a framework for learning that builds on the child's earlier experiences, helping them to develop more advanced cognitive, emotional, and social skills. The relationships and experiences that the child encounters during this period can have a lasting impact on their development, influencing their attitudes towards learning, their social relationships, and their sense of identity.

Throughout this journey of exploration, the child is continually learning and growing, developing the capacities that will support their future development and success. Each step they take, each new experience they encounter, contributes to their understanding of the world and their place within it. The process of exploration is not just about physical movement and interaction with the environment, but about the development of the mind, emotions, and identity. It is a journey of discovery that helps to shape the child's character, values, and sense of self.

Chapter 3: Family Bonds: The Foundation of Love

Family bonds, often seen as the foundational elements of human relationships, are central to the emotional, psychological, and social development of an individual. These bonds form the bedrock of one's sense of identity, security, and belonging. They shape our understanding of love, trust, and interpersonal dynamics, influencing our interactions with the world throughout our lives. Exploring the depth and breadth of family bonds reveals their pivotal role in nurturing and sustaining individuals, providing a framework for growth, resilience, and emotional well-being.

At the heart of family bonds lies the concept of attachment, a deep and enduring emotional connection that forms between a child and their caregivers. This attachment is not merely a sentimental or affectionate bond; it is a critical component of the child's development. From birth, a child depends on their caregivers for physical sustenance, protection, and emotional support. The quality of these early interactions sets the stage for the child's emotional and psychological development. A secure attachment, characterized by a caregiver's responsiveness and sensitivity, fosters a sense of trust and safety, enabling the child to explore their environment with confidence. Conversely, an insecure attachment, resulting from inconsistent or neglectful caregiving, can lead to difficulties in emotional regulation and a pervasive sense of insecurity.

Family bonds are not limited to the parent-child relationship; they extend to encompass siblings, grandparents, and other extended family members. Each of these relationships contributes uniquely to an individual's development and well-being. Sibling relationships, for instance, are often marked by a blend of companionship, rivalry, and support. These relationships provide a context for learning about cooperation, conflict resolution, and empathy. Siblings serve as playmates, confidants, and role models, offering a source of social learning that is distinct from that provided by parents. The dynamic nature of sibling relationships helps to foster a sense of belonging and continuity, as well as an understanding of social roles and family dynamics.

Grandparents and extended family members play a crucial role in the formation and maintenance of family bonds. They often provide additional layers of support, wisdom, and continuity, helping to reinforce family values and traditions. The presence of extended family can create a broader sense of community and belonging, offering children a wider network of relationships that contribute to their emotional and social development. These relationships also provide a valuable source of stability and continuity, particularly in times of stress or transition, such as during parental separation, relocation, or other significant life changes.

The role of family bonds in shaping an individual's sense of identity cannot be overstated. Family relationships provide the first context in which a child learns about themselves and their place in the world. Through interactions with family members, children develop an understanding of their own strengths, weaknesses, and unique characteristics. They also learn about their family's history, culture, and values, which helps to shape their sense of identity and belonging. The stories, traditions, and values passed down through generations contribute to a sense of continuity and connection that is integral to the formation of a stable and coherent identity.

Family bonds also play a critical role in the development of emotional intelligence. Through interactions with family members, individuals learn to recognize, understand, and manage their own emotions, as well as to empathize with the emotions of others. The emotional support provided by family members helps individuals to navigate the complexities of their own emotions and to develop effective coping strategies for dealing with stress and adversity. The ability to understand and manage emotions is a key component of emotional intelligence, which is essential for forming healthy relationships and for achieving success in various aspects of life.

The significance of family bonds extends to the realm of social development as well. Family relationships provide the first and most influential context for learning about social roles, norms, and expectations. Through interactions with family members, individuals learn about the importance of trust, cooperation, and mutual respect. They also learn about the dynamics of power and authority, as well as about the importance of empathy, compassion, and altruism. The social skills developed through family interactions form the foundation for the individual's ability to form and maintain relationships outside the family, in settings such as school, work, and the broader community.

Family bonds are also a critical source of resilience. The support and encouragement provided by family members can help individuals to overcome challenges and to cope with adversity. The sense of security and belonging provided by family relationships can serve as a buffer against stress and can help individuals to maintain a positive outlook even in difficult circumstances. The values and traditions passed down through generations can provide a source of strength and continuity, helping individuals to maintain a sense of purpose and direction in the face of adversity. The emotional support provided by family members can also help individuals to develop the coping skills and resilience needed to navigate the challenges of life.

The role of family bonds in the development of moral values and ethical behavior is also significant. Family relationships provide the first context in which individuals learn about right and wrong, about the importance of honesty, integrity, and respect for others. The values and behaviors modeled by family members help to shape the individual's own moral and ethical framework, influencing their decisions and actions throughout life. The emphasis placed on values such as kindness, generosity, and compassion within the family can have a lasting impact on the individual's character and behavior.

Family bonds also play a critical role in the development of physical and mental health. The support and care provided by family members can help to promote healthy behaviors and to prevent illness. The emotional support provided by family members can also help to protect against mental health issues such as depression and anxiety, and to promote overall well-being. The sense of security and belonging provided by family relationships can also help to reduce stress and to promote a positive outlook on life.

The impact of family bonds on an individual's development and well-being is not limited to the early years of life; it extends throughout the lifespan. Family relationships continue to provide support and guidance throughout adulthood, helping individuals to navigate the challenges of work, relationships, and parenting. The sense of connection and continuity provided by family relationships can also help individuals to maintain a positive outlook on life and to find meaning and purpose in their experiences.

Chapter 4: Childhood Joys: The Innocence of Play

Childhood joys, encapsulated in the innocence of play, form a vibrant tapestry of experiences that shape the early years of human life. These moments of pure, unadulterated joy are not merely a fleeting part of childhood; they are fundamental to the development of cognitive, emotional, and social skills that form the basis of a well-rounded individual. The innocence of play reflects the unselfconscious and spontaneous way children engage with the world, exploring their environment, relationships, and their own capabilities in ways that are both deeply fulfilling and profoundly educational. This phase of life, rich with discovery and creativity, lays the foundation for lifelong learning and emotional health.

The concept of play in childhood encompasses a wide range of activities, from solitary play to complex social interactions. It is through play that children first begin to make sense of the world around them. From the earliest moments, infants engage in exploratory play, using their senses to investigate their surroundings. They touch, taste, and observe objects, learning about their properties and how they interact with the environment. This sensory exploration is crucial for the development of neural pathways and cognitive abilities, as it helps children to understand cause and effect, spatial relationships, and object permanence.

As children grow, their play becomes more complex and imaginative. They begin to engage in symbolic play, using objects to represent other things and acting out scenarios from their daily lives. A simple block can become a car, a spaceship, or a piece of cake in the mind of a child. This type of play is not just a form of entertainment; it is a powerful tool for cognitive development. Through imaginative play, children develop their ability to think abstractly, to solve problems, and to understand the perspectives of others. They learn to negotiate rules, to cooperate, and to resolve conflicts, skills that are essential for social interaction and emotional intelligence.

The innocence of play is characterized by its spontaneity and lack of self-consciousness. Children engage in play with a sense of freedom and abandon that allows them to express themselves fully and to explore their emotions in a safe and supportive context. This freedom is essential for the development of creativity and self-expression, as it allows children to experiment with different roles, ideas, and behaviors without fear of judgment or failure. Play provides a space where children can explore their identities, test their boundaries, and discover their passions and interests.

The role of play in emotional development is also significant. Through play, children learn to recognize and understand their own emotions, as well as the emotions of others. They experience a wide range of feelings, from joy and excitement to frustration and sadness, and learn to navigate these emotions in a healthy and constructive way. Play provides a context in which children can experiment with different emotional responses, learn about empathy and compassion, and develop the skills needed to manage their emotions effectively. The joy and laughter that accompany play are not just expressions of happiness; they are essential for emotional resilience and well-being, helping children to develop a positive outlook on life and to cope with stress and adversity.

Social play, which involves interaction with peers and adults, is particularly important for the development of social skills and relationships. Through play, children learn about cooperation, sharing, and taking turns. They learn to negotiate rules, to resolve conflicts, and to work together towards common goals. These social skills are essential for forming and maintaining healthy relationships, both in childhood and later in life. Social play also provides opportunities for children to develop a sense of empathy and to understand the perspectives of others, skills that are critical for effective communication and social interaction.

The role of caregivers in supporting and facilitating play is crucial. Caregivers provide the environment, resources, and encouragement that children need to engage in meaningful play. They offer guidance and support, helping children to navigate the challenges and complexities of play, while also allowing them the freedom to explore and experiment. The involvement of caregivers in play can also strengthen the bond between parent and child, providing a context for shared experiences, communication, and mutual enjoyment. This bond is essential for the child's sense of security and well-being, and for the development of a positive self-concept.

The innocence of play also provides a context in which children can learn about their culture and the world around them. Through play, children are exposed to the values, norms, and traditions of their culture, and they learn about the roles and expectations that are associated with different social identities. This cultural learning is essential for the development of a sense of identity and belonging, and for the ability to navigate the complexities of the social world. Play also provides opportunities for children to learn about the natural world, to develop an appreciation for nature, and to understand the importance of sustainability and environmental stewardship.

The educational value of play is increasingly recognized in early childhood education. Play-based learning is an approach that emphasizes the importance of play in the development of cognitive, social, and emotional skills. Through play, children engage in activities that are both enjoyable and educational, helping them to develop the knowledge and skills they need to succeed in school and in life. Play-based learning also supports the development of a love of learning, as it encourages children to explore their interests and to engage in activities that are meaningful and relevant to their lives.

The innocence of play is not just a phase of childhood; it is a lifelong source of joy and fulfillment. The skills and experiences that children gain through play continue to benefit them throughout their lives, helping them to navigate the challenges of adulthood, to maintain healthy relationships, and to find meaning and purpose in their experiences. The sense of wonder and curiosity that characterizes play is essential for lifelong learning and personal growth, as it encourages individuals to continue to explore, to experiment, and to discover new possibilities.

Chapter 5: Lessons from Parents: Seeds of Confidence

Parents serve as the primary architects in the formative years of a child's life, laying the foundation for their confidence and self-esteem. The lessons imparted by parents, both directly and indirectly, play a crucial role in shaping a child's sense of self, their worldview, and their ability to navigate life's challenges. The concept of "Lessons from Parents: Seeds of Confidence" delves into how parental guidance, support, and modeling instill confidence in children, enabling them to develop resilience, self-assurance, and a positive self-concept. This intricate process begins in early childhood and continues to influence an individual well into adulthood, with lasting effects on their personal and professional lives.

From the earliest days of life, children look to their parents for cues about how to perceive themselves and the world around them. A parent's response to a child's needs and behaviors forms the bedrock of the child's developing self-concept and confidence. When parents respond with warmth, attentiveness, and encouragement, they communicate to the child that they are valued and capable. This foundational support is crucial in fostering a sense of security and trust, which are the first seeds of confidence. In contrast, inconsistent or negative responses can lead to feelings of insecurity and doubt, undermining a child's confidence and self-esteem.

The process of building confidence in children often begins with the establishment of a secure attachment. This bond, characterized by a parent's responsiveness and sensitivity to the child's needs, provides a safe and supportive environment in which the child can explore and grow. Securely attached children are more likely to feel confident in their abilities and to approach new experiences with a sense of curiosity and enthusiasm. They learn that they can rely on their parents for support and guidance, which in turn gives them the confidence to venture into the world and to take risks in their learning and development.

Parental modeling is another critical component in the development of confidence. Children observe and imitate the behaviors, attitudes, and values of their parents, learning about themselves and their abilities in the process. When parents model confidence and self-assurance, they provide a powerful example for their children to follow. This modeling can take many forms, from demonstrating problem-solving skills and perseverance in the face of challenges, to expressing positive self-regard and self-acceptance. By observing their parents, children learn that confidence is not about being perfect or never making mistakes, but about believing in oneself and being willing to try, learn, and grow.

The lessons that parents teach their children about coping with failure and setbacks are particularly important for the development of confidence. Life is full of challenges and obstacles, and the ability to navigate these difficulties with resilience and a positive mindset is a key aspect of confidence. Parents who model a constructive approach to failure, viewing it as an opportunity for learning and growth, help their children to develop a similar perspective. They teach their children that setbacks are a normal part of life and that they have the capacity to overcome them. This resilience in the face of adversity is a crucial component of confidence, as it enables individuals to maintain a positive self-concept and to persevere in the pursuit of their goals.

The language and feedback that parents use when interacting with their children also play a significant role in the development of confidence. Positive reinforcement, praise, and encouragement can help to build a child's self-esteem and belief in their abilities. When parents acknowledge and celebrate their children's achievements, no matter how small, they communicate a message of competence and worth. This positive feedback helps children to develop a sense of pride in their accomplishments and to feel confident in their ability to tackle new challenges. On the other hand, criticism, negative comparisons, and punitive responses can erode a child's self-confidence and lead to feelings of inadequacy and self-doubt.

Encouraging autonomy and independence is another important way that parents can foster confidence in their children. By providing opportunities for children to make choices, solve problems, and take on responsibilities, parents help their children to develop a sense of competence and self-efficacy. This autonomy supports the development of confidence, as children learn that they have the ability to influence their environment and to achieve their goals. It also helps them to develop critical thinking and decision-making skills, which are essential for confidence and self-assurance in later life.

The values and beliefs that parents impart to their children also contribute to the development of confidence. When parents instill a sense of self-worth and emphasize the importance of inner qualities such as kindness, integrity, and perseverance, they help their children to develop a strong and positive self-concept. These values provide a foundation for confidence, as they encourage children to see themselves as capable and valuable individuals. Parents who emphasize the importance of self-acceptance and self-compassion also help their children to develop a healthy and balanced sense of self-esteem, which is essential for confidence and well-being.

The role of parents in supporting their children's social development is also crucial for the development of confidence. Social skills, such as communication, empathy, and cooperation, are essential for building and maintaining relationships, and they play a significant role in an individual's overall sense of confidence and self-assurance. Parents who model and teach these skills help their children to develop the ability to interact effectively with others and to navigate social situations with confidence. This social competence is a key aspect of confidence, as it enables individuals to form positive relationships and to feel a sense of belonging and acceptance in their social circles.

The way that parents manage their own emotions and stress also has an impact on their children's confidence. Children learn a great deal about emotional regulation and coping from observing their parents. Parents who model healthy ways of managing stress and emotions, such as using coping strategies, seeking support, and maintaining a positive outlook, help their children to develop similar skills. This emotional resilience is an important component of confidence, as it enables individuals to maintain a positive self-concept and to navigate life's challenges with a sense of competence and self-assurance.

The impact of parental support and encouragement extends beyond childhood, influencing an individual's confidence and self-esteem throughout their life. The lessons learned from parents about self-worth, resilience, and competence provide a foundation for the development of a positive and enduring sense of confidence. This confidence supports individuals in their personal and professional lives, enabling them to pursue their goals, to overcome obstacles, and to achieve their potential.

Chapter 6: Friendship Blossoms: Social Beginnings

Friendship, often considered one of the most cherished aspects of human life, begins to take root during the early years of childhood and continues to evolve and flourish throughout a person's life. The development of friendships marks the beginning of a child's social journey, laying the groundwork for social skills, emotional intelligence, and a deeper understanding of human relationships. This topic, "Friendship Blossoms: Social Beginnings," explores the multifaceted nature of early friendships, their significance in personal development, and the profound impact they have on shaping an individual's social and emotional landscape.

Friendship in childhood begins with the simple act of play. It is through play that children first start to form bonds with their peers, experiencing the joy of shared activities and mutual discovery. These early friendships are often characterized by their spontaneity and simplicity. Children are drawn to one another through common interests and the desire for companionship, finding joy in each other's company without the complexities that often accompany adult relationships. This initial stage of friendship is marked by a sense of immediacy and presence, where the focus is on shared experiences and the pleasure of being together.

As children grow, their friendships begin to deepen and evolve. They move from parallel play, where they play alongside each other, to more interactive forms of play that require cooperation, negotiation, and communication. Through these interactions, children learn essential social skills such as sharing, taking turns, and resolving conflicts. They begin to understand the importance of empathy and perspective-taking, as they navigate the complexities of playing with others and accommodating different viewpoints and desires. These skills are not only crucial for forming and maintaining friendships but also for developing a broader understanding of social dynamics and human behavior.

The emotional aspect of early friendships cannot be overstated. Friendships provide a context in which children can express their emotions, explore their feelings, and receive emotional support from their peers. These relationships offer a safe space for children to experience a range of emotions, from the joy of companionship to the sadness of separation or conflict. The emotional support provided by friends helps children to develop emotional resilience, as they learn to cope with challenges and to support one another through difficult times. This emotional aspect of friendship is foundational for the development of emotional intelligence, as it helps children to understand their own emotions and to empathize with the emotions of others.

The role of friendship in the development of self-concept and identity is also significant. Through interactions with their peers, children begin to explore different aspects of their personalities and to develop a sense of who they are in relation to others. Friendships provide a context in which children can experiment with different roles and behaviors, receiving feedback from their peers that helps them to refine their self-concept and to develop a sense of identity. The acceptance and validation received from friends can boost a child's self-esteem and confidence, helping them to feel valued and understood. This process of social comparison and self-reflection is essential for the development of a stable and positive sense of self.

The significance of friendship extends beyond the individual, influencing the dynamics of the broader social group. Friendships contribute to the social cohesion and harmony of the group, as they foster a sense of belonging and mutual support. The bonds formed between friends help to create a positive and inclusive social environment, where individuals feel accepted and valued. This sense of belonging is crucial for psychological well-being, as it provides individuals with a sense of security and connectedness that supports their overall mental and emotional health.

As children progress into adolescence, friendships become even more central to their social and emotional development. During this stage of life, friendships often take on greater depth and complexity, as individuals seek out relationships that provide emotional intimacy, mutual support, and a sense of identity. Adolescents begin to place greater importance on shared values, interests, and goals, seeking out friends who can provide a sense of companionship and understanding that aligns with their evolving sense of self. These relationships become a crucial source of emotional support and validation, helping adolescents to navigate the challenges of this transitional stage of life.

The importance of loyalty and trust becomes more pronounced in adolescent friendships. Individuals begin to seek out friends who they can rely on for support, understanding, and companionship. The ability to trust and to be trusted becomes a key component of friendship, as individuals seek out relationships that provide a sense of security and stability. This emphasis on loyalty and trust helps to strengthen the bonds between friends, creating a foundation for relationships that are both enduring and fulfilling. The experiences of trust and loyalty in friendship help individuals to develop a sense of integrity and commitment, qualities that are essential for healthy and meaningful relationships.

The influence of friendships extends into adulthood, where they continue to play a crucial role in personal development and well-being. Adult friendships often take on different forms and functions, as individuals seek out relationships that provide support, companionship, and a sense of connection. These relationships can provide a valuable source of emotional support, helping individuals to cope with the challenges and stresses of adult life. The sense of belonging and acceptance provided by friendships can also support mental and emotional well-being, helping individuals to maintain a positive outlook and to feel connected and valued.

The role of friendship in promoting personal growth and self-awareness is also significant. Friendships provide a context in which individuals can explore their values, beliefs, and goals, receiving feedback and support from their peers that helps them to refine their sense of self and to develop a sense of purpose and direction. The experiences and perspectives of friends can provide valuable insights and inspiration, helping individuals to expand their horizons and to develop a deeper understanding of themselves and the world around them. The mutual support and encouragement provided by friends can also help individuals to achieve their goals and to overcome obstacles, providing a valuable source of motivation and resilience.

The importance of friendships in promoting social and community cohesion is also significant. Friendships help to build social capital, creating networks of support and cooperation that contribute to the overall well-being and stability of the community. The bonds formed between friends help to foster a sense of mutual respect and understanding, promoting social harmony and reducing conflict. The support and resources provided by friendships can also help individuals to cope with social and economic challenges, providing a valuable source of resilience and security. The role of friendship in promoting social cohesion and community well-being underscores the broader significance of these relationships, highlighting their importance not only for individual well-being but also for the health and stability of the wider society.

Chapter 7: School Days: Learning and Growing

The period known as "School Days" represents a significant chapter in the journey of human development. It is a time marked by a unique blend of structured learning, social exploration, personal growth, and the laying of foundational skills that will carry individuals throughout their lives. The experiences during school days are multifaceted, encompassing academic pursuits, social interactions, and the gradual formation of self-identity. This intricate process of learning and growing unfolds in an environment designed to foster both intellectual and personal development, providing a rich tapestry of opportunities and challenges that shape the individual in profound ways.

School days begin in early childhood, often with the transition from the familiar confines of home to the new and structured setting of a classroom. This shift represents a significant milestone, as children are introduced to a formal education system that will play a crucial role in their development. The early years of schooling are characterized by a focus on foundational skills such as literacy, numeracy, and basic social skills. These early educational experiences are designed to build a strong foundation for future learning, equipping children with the tools they need to understand and navigate the world around them.

The process of learning during school days is both systematic and exploratory. On one hand, it involves the acquisition of specific knowledge and skills, delivered through a structured curriculum that covers a wide range of subjects. Students are introduced to core areas such as language, mathematics, science, and social studies, each of which provides a different lens through which to understand the world. This structured learning is essential for the development of cognitive abilities, critical thinking skills, and the capacity to engage with complex ideas and concepts. It provides the building blocks for future academic success and lays the groundwork for lifelong learning.

On the other hand, school days also provide opportunities for exploratory learning, where students are encouraged to pursue their interests and to engage with the material in a way that is meaningful and relevant to them. This type of learning fosters curiosity and creativity, encouraging students to ask questions, to seek out new knowledge, and to explore different perspectives. It supports the development of a love of learning, as students discover the joy of exploration and the satisfaction of understanding new concepts and ideas. This balance between structured and exploratory learning is crucial for the development of a well-rounded individual, capable of thinking critically and creatively, and of adapting to new and changing circumstances.

The social aspect of school days is equally important, as it provides a context in which students can develop and refine their social skills. School is often the first setting in which children interact with a diverse group of peers, learning to navigate the complexities of social relationships and to understand the perspectives and experiences of others. These interactions provide valuable opportunities for the development of empathy, communication skills, and the ability to work collaboratively with others. Through friendships, group activities, and social interactions, students learn about cooperation, conflict resolution, and the importance of mutual respect and understanding.

The role of teachers during school days is critical, as they serve as guides, mentors, and role models for their students. Teachers provide the instruction and support needed to facilitate learning, helping students to understand new concepts, to develop their skills, and to achieve their academic goals. They also provide guidance and support for social and emotional development, helping students to navigate the challenges of school life and to develop a positive sense of self. The relationships between teachers and students are a key component of the educational experience, providing a source of support and encouragement that helps students to develop confidence and to strive for success.

The concept of "learning and growing" during school days extends beyond the acquisition of academic knowledge and social skills. It also encompasses the development of personal values, beliefs, and a sense of identity. School provides a context in which students can explore different aspects of their personalities, interests, and values, and begin to develop a sense of who they are and what they stand for. This process of self-exploration and self-discovery is essential for the development of a positive and coherent sense of identity, which supports overall well-being and resilience.

The challenges and pressures of school life also play a significant role in the process of learning and growing. The demands of academic work, the pressures of social dynamics, and the expectations of teachers and parents can create a complex and sometimes stressful environment for students. These challenges provide valuable opportunities for the development of resilience, problem-solving skills, and the ability to cope with stress and adversity. By navigating these challenges, students learn important life skills that will support them in their future endeavors and help them to overcome obstacles and achieve their goals.

The experiences of success and failure during school days are also crucial for personal growth. Successes provide a sense of achievement and validation, helping to build confidence and motivation. They reinforce the value of hard work and perseverance, and provide a sense of pride and satisfaction in one's accomplishments. Failures, on the other hand, provide valuable opportunities for learning and growth. They teach students about resilience, the importance of persistence, and the value of learning from mistakes. The ability to view failure as a learning opportunity rather than a setback is a key aspect of personal development, and is essential for the development of a growth mindset.

The extracurricular activities and opportunities provided during school days also play a significant role in the process of learning and growing. Participation in sports, arts, music, and other extracurricular activities provides valuable opportunities for the development of skills, interests, and talents. These activities help to build self-confidence, to develop teamwork and leadership skills, and to provide a sense of accomplishment and satisfaction. They also provide a context in which students can explore their interests and passions, and develop a sense of identity and purpose.

The role of the school community in supporting the process of learning and growing is also significant. The relationships and interactions within the school community, including relationships with peers, teachers, and other school staff, provide a sense of belonging and support that is crucial for overall well-being. A positive and supportive school community helps to create a safe and inclusive environment in which students can thrive, and provides a valuable source of social support and encouragement. This sense of community is essential for the development of social skills, emotional resilience, and a positive sense of self.

The transition from childhood to adolescence, and from primary to secondary education, represents a significant milestone in the journey of learning and growing. This transition brings new challenges and opportunities, as students are introduced to more complex academic subjects, greater independence, and a broader social environment. It provides a context in which students can further develop their academic skills, social relationships, and sense of identity, and prepare for the challenges and opportunities of adult life. The experiences of learning and growing during this transitional period are crucial for the development of the skills and resilience needed to navigate the complexities of the adult world.

The concept of lifelong learning, which is increasingly recognized as a key aspect of personal and professional development, is also rooted in the experiences of school days. The skills, attitudes, and habits developed during school provide the foundation for a lifelong commitment to learning and personal growth. The ability to think critically, to seek out new knowledge, and to adapt to changing circumstances are essential skills for success in the modern world, and are cultivated through the experiences of learning and growing during school days.

Chapter 8: First Failures: Handling Disappointment

The experience of failure, particularly in its earliest encounters, is a profound milestone in human development. "First Failures: Handling Disappointment" explores the complex, multifaceted process of how individuals, especially children, navigate and internalize the concept of failure and disappointment. This exploration delves into the emotional, cognitive, and social dimensions of handling setbacks and how these experiences shape one's resilience, self-perception, and future approach to challenges. Understanding how first failures are managed and integrated into a person's developmental narrative is crucial for fostering growth, resilience, and a healthy relationship with setbacks.

For many, the first brush with failure often occurs during early childhood, a period characterized by rapid learning and constant exploration. This could be as simple as struggling to complete a puzzle, not winning a game, or facing rejection from a peer. These seemingly minor disappointments play a significant role in a child's development. At this stage, children are learning not just about the external world, but also about their place within it, including their capabilities and limitations. The way in which these first failures are handled can set the tone for how individuals approach challenges and setbacks throughout their lives.

From a psychological perspective, failure is closely tied to the concept of self-efficacy, which refers to an individual's belief in their own ability to succeed in specific situations. The initial response to failure can significantly influence the development of self-efficacy. When children are supported and guided through their first failures, they learn to view these setbacks as opportunities for growth and learning rather than as reflections of their self-worth. This mindset, often referred to as a "growth mindset," encourages resilience and a willingness to embrace challenges. Conversely, if failure is met with criticism or a lack of support, children may develop a "fixed mindset," where they perceive their abilities as static and unchangeable, leading to a fear of failure and a tendency to avoid challenges.

The emotional impact of first failures is profound, as it involves navigating a range of complex feelings such as disappointment, frustration, sadness, and sometimes shame. These emotions are a natural response to unmet expectations and perceived setbacks, and learning to manage them is a crucial part of emotional development. The role of caregivers, educators, and peers is vital in helping children to process these emotions and to develop healthy coping mechanisms. By providing a supportive environment where children feel safe to express their feelings and to explore the causes and consequences of failure, adults can help to foster emotional resilience and a balanced perspective on setbacks.

A key component of handling disappointment is the development of emotional regulation skills. Emotional regulation involves the ability to manage and respond to one's emotions in a healthy and adaptive way. When children experience failure, they often need help in learning how to calm themselves, to reflect on the situation, and to find constructive ways to cope with their feelings. This might involve talking about their emotions, finding positive distractions, or engaging in problem-solving activities. These skills are essential for managing not just the immediate impact of failure, but also for developing a long-term resilience to setbacks.

The cognitive aspect of handling failure involves the development of problem-solving and critical thinking skills. When faced with failure, individuals must learn to analyze the situation, to understand what went wrong, and to identify ways to improve or to approach the problem differently in the future. This process of reflection and analysis helps to foster a mindset that views failure as a learning opportunity rather than as a dead end. It encourages individuals to take a proactive approach to challenges, to seek out new solutions, and to persist in the face of obstacles. The ability to reflect on and learn from failure is a critical skill that supports personal and academic growth, and is essential for success in all areas of life.

The social context in which failure is experienced also plays a significant role in shaping how individuals respond to and internalize setbacks. The reactions of peers, caregivers, and educators can influence a child's perception of failure and their willingness to take risks in the future. When failure is met with empathy, encouragement, and constructive feedback, it helps to build a supportive social environment that fosters resilience and a positive attitude towards challenges. Conversely, if failure is met with criticism, ridicule, or negative comparisons, it can lead to feelings of inadequacy, shame, and a fear of failure that can inhibit future risk-taking and growth.

One of the most significant long-term impacts of early failures is the development of resilience, which is the ability to recover from setbacks and to continue pursuing one's goals despite challenges. Resilience is not an innate trait, but rather a skill that can be developed through experience and support. Early experiences of failure, when managed in a supportive and constructive way, provide valuable opportunities for developing resilience. They teach individuals that setbacks are a normal part of life, that they have the ability to overcome obstacles, and that perseverance and effort are key to achieving success. This resilience is essential for navigating the complexities of life and for achieving personal and professional fulfillment.

The role of parents and caregivers in helping children to handle failure is crucial. Parents can support their children by providing a safe and nurturing environment in which to explore and learn from setbacks. This might involve offering encouragement and praise for effort rather than just for success, helping children to reflect on what they can learn from their experiences, and providing guidance and support in setting and achieving new goals. By modeling a positive and constructive approach to failure, parents can help their children to develop a healthy and resilient attitude towards challenges and setbacks.

The educational system also plays a significant role in shaping how individuals handle failure and disappointment. Schools can create a learning environment that encourages a growth mindset, where failure is viewed as a natural part of the learning process and as an opportunity for growth and improvement. This might involve providing opportunities for students to take risks and to learn from their mistakes, offering constructive feedback and support, and promoting a culture of perseverance and resilience. By fostering a positive and supportive learning environment, schools can help students to develop the skills and mindset needed to handle failure and to succeed in all areas of life.

As individuals grow and mature, their experiences of failure continue to shape their approach to challenges and setbacks. Adolescence and adulthood bring new and more complex challenges, from academic pressures and social dynamics to career ambitions and personal goals. The lessons learned from early experiences of failure provide a foundation for navigating these challenges with resilience and confidence. By building on their experiences of failure and learning from their mistakes, individuals can continue to grow and to develop the skills and mindset needed to achieve their goals and to lead fulfilling and successful lives.

Chapter 9: Sibling Rivalry: Navigating Family Dynamics

Sibling rivalry, an age-old dynamic observed across cultures and societies, is a complex phenomenon that plays a crucial role in the development of interpersonal skills, emotional resilience, and individual identity. The term "sibling rivalry" encompasses a range of behaviors, from competition and jealousy to companionship and collaboration, all of which are essential in navigating family dynamics. This intricate relationship can shape a person's character, influence their social interactions, and provide a unique context for personal growth. Understanding the nuances of sibling rivalry is vital for appreciating its impact on family life and the individual development of each sibling.

At its core, sibling rivalry originates from a fundamental human need for attention, recognition, and validation. This need becomes particularly pronounced within the family context, where siblings vie for the affection, approval, and resources of their parents. This competition is not inherently negative; rather, it reflects a natural and necessary part of growing up. It is through these interactions that siblings learn to negotiate, compete, and collaborate, developing a range of skills that are critical for their social and emotional development.

The dynamics of sibling rivalry are influenced by various factors, including birth order, age differences, and gender. Birth order can play a significant role in shaping the nature of sibling interactions. Firstborn children, for example, often experience a period of undivided parental attention before the arrival of younger siblings. This can lead to a sense of entitlement and responsibility, as well as anxiety about losing their parents' attention. Younger siblings, on the other hand, may feel pressure to compete for attention and to establish their own unique identity within the family. They may also benefit from the experience and guidance of their older siblings, which can mitigate feelings of competition.

Age differences between siblings can also affect the nature of rivalry. Siblings who are close in age may compete more directly with one another for parental attention and resources, as they are likely to share similar interests and developmental stages. This can lead to more intense rivalry, but also to a deeper bond and mutual understanding. Siblings with a larger age gap, while potentially experiencing less direct competition, may struggle with feelings of isolation or a lack of common ground. These dynamics can influence the nature of their relationship and the ways in which they interact and support each other.

Gender can also influence sibling rivalry, as societal expectations and family dynamics often play a role in shaping the relationships between siblings of different genders. Brothers and sisters may experience different types of competition and conflict, based on gender roles and expectations. For example, brothers may compete more directly in areas such as sports or academic achievement, while sisters may experience rivalry in social or emotional domains. Mixed-gender sibling pairs may navigate different types of rivalry, balancing competition with the desire to support and protect each other. These gender dynamics can add an additional layer of complexity to sibling relationships, influencing the ways in which siblings interact and support one another.

The role of parents in managing sibling rivalry is critical. Parents can influence the dynamics of sibling relationships in numerous ways, from the way they distribute attention and resources to the strategies they use to resolve conflicts. Consistent and fair treatment of each child can help to reduce feelings of competition and jealousy, while providing opportunities for each child to develop their own unique talents and interests. Parental strategies for managing conflict, such as encouraging open communication and teaching problem-solving skills, can also play a significant role in shaping the nature of sibling rivalry and fostering healthy relationships between siblings.

One of the most significant aspects of sibling rivalry is its role in the development of social and emotional skills. Through their interactions with siblings, children learn to navigate complex social dynamics, to manage conflict, and to develop empathy and understanding. Sibling rivalry provides a unique context in which children can practice negotiating, compromising, and resolving conflicts in a safe and supportive environment. These skills are essential for success in all areas of life, from personal relationships to professional endeavors.

The emotional impact of sibling rivalry can be profound, influencing an individual's self-esteem, sense of identity, and emotional resilience. Siblings often compare themselves to one another, measuring their own achievements and abilities against those of their brothers and sisters. This process of comparison can lead to feelings of inadequacy or jealousy, but it can also motivate individuals to strive for their own personal best. The emotional support provided by siblings, despite the rivalry, can also play a significant role in developing emotional resilience and a positive self-concept.

Sibling rivalry can also influence the development of individual identity. The desire to stand out and to be recognized as unique can lead siblings to develop their own interests, talents, and areas of expertise. This process of differentiation can help individuals to build a strong sense of identity and to develop a sense of self-worth that is independent of their siblings. The experience of navigating rivalry and competition can also foster a sense of independence and self-reliance, as individuals learn to pursue their own goals and to assert their own needs and desires.

The positive aspects of sibling rivalry often outweigh the negative, providing valuable opportunities for personal growth and development. The challenges and conflicts inherent in sibling relationships can help individuals to develop a range of skills and qualities, from resilience and perseverance to empathy and cooperation. The experience of navigating rivalry and competition can also foster a sense of resilience and a willingness to embrace challenges, qualities that are essential for success in all areas of life.

Sibling rivalry does not end with childhood, but continues to evolve and change throughout an individual's life. As siblings grow older, their relationships often become more complex and multifaceted, reflecting changes in their personal lives, careers, and social roles. The dynamics of sibling rivalry can shift as individuals move through different life stages, from adolescence and young adulthood to middle age and beyond. These changes can influence the nature of sibling relationships and the ways in which individuals navigate rivalry and competition.

In adulthood, sibling rivalry can manifest in different ways, from competition over career achievements and financial success to conflicts over family responsibilities and inheritance issues. The dynamics of sibling rivalry can also be influenced by the changing roles and responsibilities of each sibling, such as the care of aging parents or the support of other family members. Despite these challenges, the bonds between siblings often remain strong, providing a source of support, companionship, and mutual understanding that can enrich an individual's life.

The role of sibling relationships in supporting overall well-being is also significant. Siblings can provide a valuable source of emotional support, offering understanding and empathy that is rooted in a shared family history and experience. The bonds between siblings can provide a sense of continuity and stability, helping individuals to navigate the challenges and changes of life. The support and companionship provided by siblings can also play a significant role in promoting mental and emotional well-being, helping individuals to cope with stress and adversity and to achieve a sense of fulfillment and satisfaction.

The influence of sibling rivalry on family dynamics is profound, shaping the relationships between family members and influencing the overall functioning of the family unit. The dynamics of sibling rivalry can affect the way in which family members interact, communicate, and resolve conflicts, influencing the overall cohesion and stability of the family. The management of sibling rivalry can also play a significant role in promoting a positive and supportive family environment, helping to foster healthy relationships and to support the well-being of all family members.

The impact of sibling rivalry on an individual's personal and social development is significant, shaping their approach to relationships, their sense of identity, and their overall well-being. The experience of navigating rivalry and competition with siblings provides valuable opportunities for the development of social and emotional skills, resilience, and a positive sense of self. The support and companionship provided by siblings can also play a significant role in promoting mental and emotional well-being, helping individuals to navigate the challenges of life and to achieve a sense of fulfillment and satisfaction.

Chapter 10: Imaginary Worlds: The Power of Creativity

Imaginary worlds represent a profound aspect of human creativity, offering a rich tapestry where imagination and reality intertwine. These worlds are not mere flights of fancy; they serve as fertile grounds for exploration, expression, and the development of cognitive and emotional skills. From childhood fantasies to adult artistic creations, imaginary worlds play a pivotal role in shaping individual identity, fostering innovation, and providing a sanctuary for dreams and aspirations.

At its essence, the creation of imaginary worlds is a testament to the human capacity for abstract thought and creativity. It begins in early childhood, where children effortlessly weave together elements from their surroundings—be it toys, books, or nature—to construct elaborate realms where anything is possible. These worlds often serve as safe havens where children can explore their emotions, experiment with different roles and scenarios, and make sense of the complexities of the world around them. Whether it's pretending to be superheroes saving the world or princes and princesses in enchanted castles, these imaginative play scenarios lay the groundwork for creative thinking and problem-solving skills.

Imaginary worlds are not confined to childhood play; they extend into various forms of artistic expression across cultures and ages. Literature, for instance, is replete with imaginary worlds—from J.R.R. Tolkien's Middle-earth to J.K. Rowling's wizarding world of Harry Potter—where authors create entire universes complete with histories, languages, and cultures. These fictional realms serve not only as entertainment but also as mirrors that reflect and critique aspects of our own reality. They provide readers with a lens through which to explore complex themes, grapple with moral dilemmas, and contemplate the human condition.

Similarly, visual arts, such as painting, sculpture, and digital media, often depict imaginary worlds that stretch the boundaries of the possible. Artists use their creative vision to transport viewers to fantastical landscapes, surreal dreamscapes, or futuristic cityscapes that challenge perceptions and inspire awe. These artworks invite contemplation, evoke emotions, and spark imagination, offering viewers a glimpse into the artist's unique perspective and inviting them to interpret and connect with the work on a personal level.

In cinema and animation, imaginary worlds come to life through the magic of storytelling and visual effects. Filmmakers and animators harness the power of technology to create immersive worlds that captivate audiences and transport them to realms beyond their everyday experiences. From epic space operas to whimsical animated fantasies, these films allow viewers to suspend disbelief and immerse themselves in narratives that celebrate the limitless possibilities of human imagination.

The allure of imaginary worlds lies not only in their ability to entertain but also in their potential to inspire innovation and exploration. Science fiction, for example, often extrapolates current scientific knowledge to envision future technologies, societies, and worlds. Authors like Isaac Asimov and Arthur C. Clarke have imagined space travel, artificial intelligence, and other scientific advancements long before they became realities, influencing scientists, engineers, and inventors to strive towards turning fiction into fact.

Moreover, imaginary worlds serve as catalysts for personal growth and self-discovery. Engaging with these worlds allows individuals to explore different perspectives, empathize with characters from diverse backgrounds, and confront moral dilemmas in a safe and controlled environment. This process of imaginative engagement fosters empathy, critical thinking, and emotional intelligence—skills that are essential for navigating the complexities of modern life and forming meaningful connections with others.

The act of creating imaginary worlds also holds therapeutic value. For many, writing stories, composing music, painting scenes, or crafting digital landscapes serves as a form of catharsis—a way to process emotions, heal from trauma, and explore aspects of the self that may be difficult to articulate through words alone. Through creative expression, individuals can confront their fears, confront their fears, and envision possibilities for personal transformation and growth.

In educational settings, imaginary worlds play a vital role in stimulating curiosity, enhancing learning outcomes, and fostering creativity. Teachers often use storytelling, role-playing, and interactive simulations to make complex subjects more accessible and engaging for students. By immersing learners in fictional scenarios or historical reenactments, educators encourage active participation, critical thinking, and collaboration—all while cultivating a deeper understanding of academic concepts and real-world issues.

The significance of imaginary worlds extends beyond individual creativity to encompass cultural and societal impacts. Folklore, mythology, and religious narratives are foundational examples of imaginary worlds that have shaped beliefs, rituals, and societal norms throughout history. These narratives provide frameworks for understanding the world, explaining natural phenomena, and transmitting cultural values from one generation to the next. They serve as repositories of collective wisdom, offering insights into human experiences, aspirations, and aspirations.

Moreover, imaginary worlds often serve as platforms for social commentary and political critique. Artists, writers, and filmmakers use fictional narratives to challenge prevailing ideologies, expose social injustices, and envision alternative futures. Through dystopian fiction, for example, authors explore the consequences of unchecked power, societal inequality, and environmental degradation, prompting readers to reflect on current issues and consider pathways towards a more just and sustainable world.

45

Chapter 11: Teenage Turmoil: The Search for Identity

Teenage turmoil, often marked by the search for identity, is a significant phase in human development. This period is characterized by a multitude of physical, emotional, and psychological changes that collectively contribute to the shaping of an individual's personality and sense of self. Adolescents grapple with the challenges of transitioning from childhood to adulthood, striving to understand who they are and where they fit into the world around them.

During the teenage years, individuals experience rapid physical growth and hormonal changes, which can lead to a heightened awareness of their bodies and a preoccupation with their appearance. This newfound self-consciousness often sparks an intense need for acceptance and belonging, as teenagers seek validation from their peers. Peer relationships become paramount, and the desire to fit in can drive adolescents to conform to group norms, sometimes at the expense of their own values and beliefs.

The quest for identity during adolescence is also deeply intertwined with cognitive development. Teenagers begin to develop the ability to think abstractly and critically, questioning established norms and exploring different ideologies. This cognitive shift allows them to consider various possibilities for their future, ponder existential questions, and reflect on their values and goals. As they explore different aspects of their identity, they may experiment with different roles and behaviors, trying on various "selves" to see which ones resonate most authentically.

Family dynamics play a crucial role in shaping an adolescent's identity. While parents and caregivers provide the initial framework for a child's sense of self, the teenage years often involve a reevaluation of these early influences. Adolescents may challenge parental authority and seek greater autonomy, leading to conflicts and a renegotiation of family relationships. Despite these tensions, a supportive and understanding family environment can provide a stable foundation for teenagers as they navigate the complexities of identity formation.

Cultural and societal influences also significantly impact the search for identity. Adolescents are exposed to a wide array of cultural norms, media messages, and societal expectations that can shape their perceptions of themselves and their aspirations. Social media, in particular, plays a powerful role in contemporary teenage life, offering both opportunities for self-expression and challenges related to self-esteem and body image. The pressure to curate a perfect online persona can exacerbate feelings of inadequacy and contribute to the turmoil of identity formation.

Psychological factors, such as temperament and personality traits, further influence how teenagers navigate their search for identity. Some adolescents may approach this journey with confidence and resilience, while others may struggle with self-doubt and anxiety. The interplay between an individual's innate characteristics and their experiences can lead to diverse outcomes in the development of identity. For instance, a teenager with a strong sense of self-worth may be more likely to resist peer pressure and stay true to their values, while one with lower self-esteem may be more susceptible to external influences.

The search for identity is not a linear process; it often involves periods of confusion, experimentation, and reevaluation. Adolescents may oscillate between different identities before arriving at a more cohesive sense of self. This process can be fraught with emotional ups and downs, as teenagers grapple with uncertainty and the fear of not living up to their own or others' expectations. However, these challenges are also opportunities for growth and self-discovery, as adolescents learn to navigate the complexities of their inner and outer worlds.

One of the critical tasks of adolescence is the development of a coherent narrative about oneself. This involves integrating various aspects of one's identity, such as personal values, beliefs, and goals, into a unified sense of self. Adolescents must reconcile their past experiences with their present realities and future aspirations, creating a story that makes sense of their journey and provides a sense of continuity. This narrative construction is essential for establishing a stable and enduring identity that can guide them through adulthood.

Education and extracurricular activities can also play a pivotal role in the search for identity. Schools provide a structured environment where adolescents can explore their interests, develop skills, and form relationships outside the family context. Participation in sports, arts, clubs, and other activities allows teenagers to discover their passions and strengths, contributing to a more nuanced understanding of themselves. Positive experiences in these domains can enhance self-esteem and provide a sense of purpose and direction.

The search for identity during adolescence is influenced by the broader social and historical context. Events such as economic downturns, political upheaval, and cultural shifts can impact the opportunities available to teenagers and shape their aspirations. For example, growing up in an era of technological advancement and globalization may lead adolescents to develop identities that are more interconnected and cosmopolitan. Conversely, periods of social instability and uncertainty can heighten the challenges of identity formation, as teenagers navigate a rapidly changing world.

Relationships with mentors and role models can also be crucial in the search for identity. Teachers, coaches, community leaders, and other influential adults can provide guidance, support, and inspiration, helping adolescents to envision possibilities for their future selves. Positive role models can demonstrate the values and behaviors that contribute to a healthy and fulfilling identity, while also offering practical advice and encouragement. These relationships can be especially important for teenagers who may lack supportive family environments or face other significant challenges.

The search for identity is a deeply personal and individual journey, but it is also a universal aspect of human development. While the specific experiences and challenges may vary, the fundamental quest to understand oneself and one's place in the world is a common thread that unites adolescents across different cultures and backgrounds. This shared aspect of the human experience underscores the importance of providing supportive environments that foster self-exploration and personal growth during this critical period.

Chapter 12: Peer Pressure: The Struggle to Fit In

Peer pressure, a potent force in the lives of adolescents, profoundly shapes their behavior, choices, and sense of identity. This phenomenon is characterized by the influence that peers exert on each other to conform to group norms, expectations, and behaviors. The struggle to fit in, driven by peer pressure, is a complex and multifaceted experience that can have both positive and negative consequences on an individual's development and well-being.

Adolescence is a time when social interactions and peer relationships become increasingly important. As teenagers seek to establish their independence from their families, they turn to their peers for acceptance, validation, and a sense of belonging. This shift in focus from family to peer group is a natural part of development, but it also opens the door to the powerful sway of peer pressure. The desire to be accepted by one's peers can lead adolescents to adopt behaviors and attitudes that they might not otherwise choose, as they navigate the delicate balance between individuality and conformity.

The impact of peer pressure can be seen in various aspects of teenage life, from clothing choices and hobbies to more significant decisions about substance use, academic performance, and social behavior. For instance, teenagers may feel compelled to wear certain styles of clothing, listen to particular types of music, or participate in specific activities to align with their peer group's preferences. These surface-level manifestations of peer pressure, while often harmless, underscore the deeper need for social acceptance and the fear of being ostracized or ridiculed.

However, peer pressure can also lead to more serious and potentially harmful behaviors. Adolescents may experiment with alcohol, drugs, or risky behaviors as a way to gain approval or avoid rejection from their peers. The pressure to engage in these activities can be intense, especially if the peer group values these behaviors as markers of maturity, independence, or popularity. The struggle to fit in can override an individual's better judgment, leading them to make choices that jeopardize their health, safety, and future prospects.

Academic performance is another area where peer pressure can exert a significant influence. Teenagers may feel pressured to achieve high grades and excel in extracurricular activities to meet the expectations of their peers, parents, and teachers. Conversely, they may also experience pressure to downplay their academic achievements or engage in behaviors like skipping classes and neglecting schoolwork to fit in with a peer group that values rebellion or disengagement. This dichotomy highlights the complex ways in which peer pressure can both motivate and hinder academic success.

The struggle to fit in is further complicated by the advent of social media, which amplifies the reach and intensity of peer pressure. Platforms like Instagram, Snapchat, and TikTok allow teenagers to curate and share their lives in real-time, creating a constant stream of comparison and competition. The desire to present a perfect online persona can lead to feelings of inadequacy, anxiety, and depression, as adolescents measure themselves against the often idealized and filtered images of their peers. The fear of missing out (FOMO) can drive teenagers to participate in activities or adopt behaviors they might otherwise avoid, simply to keep up with their peers' social lives.

Despite the challenges associated with peer pressure, it is important to recognize that it can also have positive effects. Peer groups can provide support, encouragement, and a sense of community, helping teenagers to develop confidence and self-esteem. Positive peer pressure can motivate adolescents to adopt healthy behaviors, such as participating in sports, volunteering, or pursuing academic excellence. When peer groups promote constructive values and behaviors, they can serve as a powerful force for good in an adolescent's life.

Understanding the dynamics of peer pressure requires an examination of the psychological and social factors at play. Adolescents are at a stage of development where their brains are particularly attuned to social signals and rewards. The regions of the brain involved in processing social information and emotions are highly active, making teenagers especially sensitive to peer approval and rejection. This heightened sensitivity can make peer pressure feel overwhelmingly powerful, as the desire to fit in and be liked takes precedence over other considerations.

Family background and parenting styles also play a crucial role in how adolescents respond to peer pressure. Supportive and communicative family environments can provide a strong foundation for teenagers to develop a healthy sense of self and resilience against negative peer influences. When parents and caregivers foster open dialogue, set clear expectations, and model positive behaviors, they equip their children with the tools to navigate peer pressure effectively. Conversely, a lack of support or overly authoritarian parenting can leave adolescents more vulnerable to the negative aspects of peer pressure.

Schools and community organizations can also play a pivotal role in addressing the challenges of peer pressure. Educational programs that promote social-emotional learning, critical thinking, and decision-making skills can empower adolescents to make informed choices and resist negative peer influences. Extracurricular activities and peer mentoring programs can provide positive role models and create environments where healthy peer relationships can flourish. By fostering a culture of inclusivity and respect, schools and communities can help mitigate the detrimental effects of peer pressure.

Peer pressure is not limited to adolescence; it can continue to influence behavior and decision-making into adulthood. However, the foundations laid during the teenage years can have a lasting impact on how individuals handle social influences throughout their lives.

Developing a strong sense of self, confidence in one's values, and the ability to make independent decisions are crucial skills that can help individuals navigate peer pressure at any stage of life.

The struggle to fit in and the influence of peer pressure are universal experiences that transcend cultural and socioeconomic boundaries. While the specific manifestations of peer pressure may vary, the underlying dynamics of social influence and the desire for acceptance are consistent across different contexts. This universality underscores the importance of addressing peer pressure as a critical aspect of adolescent development and mental health.

Chapter 13: First Love: Heartbeats and Heartbreaks

First love is a profound and unforgettable experience that often marks a significant milestone in a person's life. It is a time filled with intense emotions, excitement, and discovery, as well as vulnerability and potential heartbreak. The journey of first love, with its heartbeats and heartbreaks, plays a crucial role in shaping an individual's understanding of relationships, self-worth, and emotional resilience.

For many, the experience of first love begins in adolescence, a period already fraught with change and self-discovery. The physical and emotional changes occurring during this time can amplify the intensity of romantic feelings. The initial stirrings of attraction can be thrilling and bewildering, as teenagers navigate the complexities of these new emotions. The first time a person experiences the flutter of heartbeats at the sight of their beloved, it feels like a magical and transformative moment, signaling the beginning of an exciting new chapter in life.

First love often involves a heightened sense of idealism and passion. Adolescents tend to view their first romantic relationship through a lens of idealized perfection, projecting their hopes and dreams onto their partner. This idealization can lead to an intense emotional connection, where every moment shared feels extraordinary. The euphoria of mutual affection, the joy of holding hands for the first time, and the thrill of shared secrets and laughter create memories that linger long after the relationship has ended.

The experience of first love is not only about the joy of connection but also about the profound self-discovery that comes with it. As individuals navigate their feelings and interactions with their first love, they learn about their own desires, boundaries, and vulnerabilities. This process of self-discovery is essential for personal growth, as it helps individuals understand what they value in a relationship and what they need to feel loved and respected.

However, the intensity of first love also makes it particularly susceptible to heartbreak. The same idealism that fuels the euphoria of first love can lead to unrealistic expectations and disappointment. When the relationship encounters challenges or ends, the pain can be overwhelming. The first experience of romantic rejection or betrayal can shatter the sense of security and invincibility that often accompanies first love, leaving individuals feeling vulnerable and heartbroken.

The heartbreak of first love is a universal experience, yet it is deeply personal and unique for each individual. The emotional pain can be intense, marked by feelings of loss, sadness, and confusion. For many, the end of first love can feel like the end of the world, as they grapple with the loss of their partner and the future they had imagined together. This heartbreak can be compounded by the sense of losing a part of oneself, as first love often becomes intertwined with one's identity and sense of self-worth.

Despite the pain, the heartbreak of first love also offers valuable lessons and opportunities for growth. It teaches individuals about resilience and the capacity to heal from emotional wounds. Through the process of mourning and moving on from first love, individuals learn to navigate their emotions, develop coping mechanisms, and rebuild their sense of self. This emotional resilience is a crucial skill that will serve them in future relationships and throughout life.

First love also provides a reference point for future romantic relationships. The lessons learned from the joys and sorrows of first love inform how individuals approach subsequent relationships. They gain a clearer understanding of what they want and need in a partner, as well as what they are willing to compromise on. The memories of first love, both good and bad, shape their expectations and behaviors in future romantic endeavors, helping them make more informed and mature decisions.

Moreover, the experience of first love can foster empathy and compassion. Having gone through the highs and lows of a romantic relationship, individuals are better equipped to understand and support others who are experiencing similar emotions. This empathy can enhance their ability to form deep and meaningful connections with others, both romantically and platonically.

The cultural and social context in which first love occurs also plays a significant role in shaping the experience. Cultural norms and societal expectations influence how individuals perceive and navigate their first romantic relationships. In some cultures, first love is celebrated and encouraged, while in others, it may be viewed with caution or even disapproval. These cultural influences can impact how individuals express their love, manage their emotions, and cope with heartbreak.

In addition to cultural factors, family dynamics and upbringing also affect the experience of first love. Supportive and open family environments can provide a safe space for individuals to explore their romantic feelings and seek guidance when needed. Conversely, restrictive or unsupportive family environments can add stress and complicate the experience of first love. The way parents and caregivers respond to their children's romantic relationships can significantly influence how those relationships unfold and how the individuals involved cope with the associated emotions.

The role of media and popular culture in shaping perceptions of first love cannot be underestimated. Movies, books, and music often romanticize first love, portraying it as an all-consuming and perfect experience. While these portrayals can be inspiring, they can also set unrealistic expectations and contribute to the idealization of first love. When reality falls short of these expectations, it can lead to disappointment and disillusionment. However, media can also provide valuable insights and comfort, helping individuals feel less alone in their experiences of love and heartbreak.

Technology and social media have added new dimensions to the experience of first love in contemporary society. The ability to connect and communicate instantly has changed the dynamics of romantic relationships. While technology can facilitate closeness and intimacy, it can also introduce new challenges, such as the pressure to maintain a perfect online image or the difficulty of navigating digital communication during conflicts. Social media can amplify the highs and lows of first love, making the joys more public and the heartbreak more visible.

Despite the evolving landscape of first love in the digital age, the core emotions and experiences remain timeless. The exhilaration of first love, the depth of the emotional connection, and the pain of heartbreak are universal experiences that transcend time and technological advances. These experiences are a fundamental part of the human condition, shaping how individuals understand love, relationships, and themselves.

Chapter 14: Academic Pressure: The Weight of Expectations

Academic pressure, the weight of expectations from various sources including parents, teachers, society, and oneself, is a pervasive and significant force in the lives of students. This pressure can have profound impacts on their mental, emotional, and physical well-being. The intricate dynamics of academic pressure reflect the complexity of modern education systems, the value placed on academic achievement, and the broader societal expectations regarding success and future prospects.

From an early age, students are introduced to the concept of academic success as a primary indicator of their potential and worth. Parents, often driven by the desire to see their children succeed and secure a prosperous future, can place considerable emphasis on academic performance. This expectation can manifest in various ways, from encouraging high grades and rigorous study habits to enrolling children in extracurricular activities designed to enhance their academic profiles. While the intention is to support and motivate, the pressure can sometimes be overwhelming, leading to a sense of inadequacy and stress if the desired results are not achieved.

Schools and teachers also play a significant role in shaping academic pressure. The educational system, with its focus on standardized testing, grades, and measurable outcomes, often prioritizes academic achievement over other aspects of personal development. Students are frequently assessed and ranked based on their performance, which can create a competitive environment. This competition can drive students to push themselves harder, sometimes at the expense of their mental and physical health. Teachers, too, may feel the pressure to ensure their students perform well, which can inadvertently be transferred to the students.

Societal expectations further exacerbate academic pressure. In many cultures, academic success is equated with intelligence, discipline, and potential for future success. This societal valuation places a heavy burden on students to excel academically to secure their place in prestigious universities and, subsequently, in the job market. The narrative that a successful career and a fulfilling life are contingent upon academic excellence adds to the already considerable weight of expectations. Media and popular culture often reinforce these ideals, showcasing stories of exceptional academic achievers as role models, which can set unrealistic standards for many students.

The internalization of these external pressures leads to self-imposed expectations, where students develop a personal drive to meet or exceed the standards set by others. This self-driven pressure can be beneficial in moderation, fostering discipline, resilience, and a strong work ethic. However, when it becomes excessive, it can lead to negative consequences such as anxiety, depression, burnout, and a diminished sense of self-worth. The fear of failure and the need to continually prove oneself can create a relentless cycle of stress and pressure.

The impact of academic pressure is multifaceted and can vary significantly among individuals. For some, it can be a motivating force that drives them to achieve their full potential. These students might thrive under pressure, using it as a catalyst for their success. They may develop effective coping mechanisms, time management skills, and a strong sense of purpose. For others, however, the pressure can be debilitating, leading to mental health issues, disengagement from learning, and a decrease in overall well-being. The disparity in how students handle academic pressure often depends on various factors, including personality traits, support systems, and individual resilience.

Mental health is one of the most critical areas affected by academic pressure. The constant stress of meeting high expectations can lead to anxiety disorders, depression, and other mental health issues. Students may experience symptoms such as insomnia, fatigue, irritability, and a sense of hopelessness. The fear of disappointing parents, teachers, or themselves can create a significant emotional burden. In severe cases, the pressure can lead to extreme outcomes such as self-harm or suicidal thoughts. It is essential for educational institutions and families to recognize the signs of stress and provide appropriate support to students struggling with academic pressure.

The physical health of students can also be compromised by academic pressure. The stress associated with high expectations can lead to a range of physical symptoms, including headaches, stomach issues, and weakened immune systems. The long hours spent studying and the lack of adequate rest and relaxation can result in chronic fatigue and burnout. Additionally, students may neglect other aspects of their health, such as proper nutrition and physical activity, as they prioritize academic tasks over their well-being.

Academic pressure also affects students' social lives and relationships. The time and energy devoted to meeting academic expectations can limit opportunities for social interaction and the development of meaningful relationships. Students may feel isolated or disconnected from their peers, as their focus on academic success can create a sense of distance. The competitive nature of academic environments can also lead to tension and rivalry among students, further impacting their social dynamics. Building a supportive network of friends and mentors can be challenging when academic pressure dominates one's life.

Despite these challenges, there are strategies that students, families, and educational institutions can employ to mitigate the negative effects of academic pressure. Open communication between parents and children is crucial in understanding and addressing the pressures faced by students. Parents should strive to create a supportive and nurturing environment where academic achievements are celebrated, but not at the expense of the child's overall well-being. Encouraging a balanced approach to education, where effort and improvement are valued alongside grades and test scores, can help reduce the sense of overwhelming pressure.

Educational institutions can play a pivotal role in alleviating academic pressure by promoting a more holistic approach to learning. Schools should emphasize the importance of mental and emotional health, integrating wellness programs and stress management techniques into the curriculum. Providing resources such as counseling services, peer support groups, and workshops on time management and study skills can help students develop healthy coping mechanisms. Creating a school culture that values diverse talents and abilities, rather than solely academic achievements, can foster a more inclusive and supportive environment.

Society at large can contribute to reducing academic pressure by redefining the metrics of success. While academic achievement is important, it should not be the sole determinant of a person's worth or potential. Recognizing and celebrating diverse paths to success, including vocational training, creative pursuits, and entrepreneurial endeavors, can broaden the perspective on what it means to be successful. Media and popular culture can play a role by showcasing a variety of success stories, highlighting the importance of resilience, adaptability, and personal fulfillment.

On an individual level, students can develop strategies to manage academic pressure and maintain a healthy balance in their lives. Practicing self-care, such as regular physical activity, adequate sleep, and relaxation techniques, can help mitigate the effects of stress. Setting realistic goals and prioritizing tasks can improve time management and reduce the sense of being overwhelmed. Building a strong support network of friends, family, and mentors can provide emotional support and practical advice. Seeking professional help when needed, such as counseling or therapy, can also be beneficial in managing the mental health impacts of academic pressure.

Chapter 15: Body Image: Facing the Mirror

Body image, the perception and attitudes one has towards their physical appearance, is a deeply personal and often complex issue that affects people of all ages, genders, and backgrounds. The way individuals perceive their bodies can significantly impact their self-esteem, mental health, and overall well-being. In contemporary society, where media and cultural standards heavily influence perceptions of beauty, facing the mirror can be a challenging and sometimes distressing experience.

From an early age, individuals are bombarded with images and messages that shape their understanding of what is considered attractive or desirable. These messages come from various sources, including family, peers, media, and popular culture. The idealized body types presented in advertisements, television shows, movies, and social media often set unrealistic standards that are difficult, if not impossible, for most people to achieve. This pervasive exposure to idealized images can lead to dissatisfaction with one's own body and the development of negative body image.

The formation of body image begins in childhood and is influenced by family dynamics and early experiences. Children often learn attitudes towards body image from their parents or caregivers. For instance, a parent's comments about their own body or their child's appearance can have a lasting impact. Positive reinforcement and a focus on health rather than appearance can foster a healthy body image, while critical remarks or an emphasis on weight and appearance can contribute to body dissatisfaction. Additionally, the way parents respond to societal pressures and media representations of beauty can model critical thinking and resilience for their children.

As individuals grow older, peer influences become increasingly significant in shaping body image. Adolescence, in particular, is a critical period for body image development, as young people are navigating physical changes, social dynamics, and identity formation. Peer pressure and the desire for acceptance can drive adolescents to compare themselves to their peers and strive to meet perceived standards of attractiveness. Bullying, teasing, or exclusion based on appearance can have devastating effects on a young person's self-esteem and body image.

Media and popular culture play a powerful role in shaping societal standards of beauty and influencing individual body image. The portrayal of idealized body types in fashion magazines, television shows, movies, and social media creates a narrow definition of beauty that often excludes the diversity of real bodies. These media representations frequently emphasize thinness for women and muscularity for men, perpetuating stereotypes and unrealistic expectations. The use of photo editing and filters to enhance or alter appearances further distorts reality, making it even harder for individuals to feel satisfied with their natural bodies.

Social media has amplified the impact of media on body image by creating a platform for constant comparison and validation. Platforms like Instagram, TikTok, and Snapchat allow users to curate and share their lives, often presenting an idealized version of reality. The pressure to gain likes, followers, and positive comments can lead individuals to prioritize appearance and seek validation through their looks. This constant comparison to others, who may also be presenting an edited or filtered version of themselves, can exacerbate feelings of inadequacy and body dissatisfaction.

The impact of body image on mental health is profound. Negative body image is associated with a range of psychological issues, including low self-esteem, depression, anxiety, and eating disorders. Individuals who are dissatisfied with their bodies may engage in unhealthy behaviors such as extreme dieting, over-exercising, or disordered eating in an attempt to change their appearance. These behaviors can have serious physical and psychological consequences, further perpetuating the cycle of negative body image and poor mental health.

Eating disorders, such as anorexia nervosa, bulimia nervosa, and binge-eating disorder, are severe manifestations of body image issues. These disorders involve distorted perceptions of body size and shape, an intense fear of gaining weight, and harmful behaviors related to food and eating. The causes of eating disorders are multifaceted, involving genetic, psychological, and environmental factors, but societal pressures and cultural standards of beauty play a significant role. Early intervention and comprehensive treatment are crucial for individuals struggling with eating disorders, as these conditions can be life-threatening if left untreated.

Body image issues are not limited to women; men also face societal pressures and unrealistic standards regarding their bodies. The idealized image of the muscular, lean male body is pervasive in media and popular culture, leading many men to feel inadequate or dissatisfied with their appearance. This pressure can result in behaviors such as excessive exercising, the use of supplements or steroids, and disordered eating patterns. Men may also struggle with discussing their body image concerns due to societal stigmas around expressing vulnerability and emotions.

Cultural and ethnic differences add another layer of complexity to body image. Different cultures have varying standards of beauty, and individuals from diverse backgrounds may experience conflicting pressures to conform to multiple ideals. For instance, Western beauty standards often emphasize thinness and fair skin, which can clash with the traditional beauty ideals of other cultures that may value curves or darker skin tones. Navigating these conflicting messages can be challenging and can impact an individual's body image and sense of identity.

Body positivity and acceptance movements have emerged in response to the pervasive impact of negative body image and societal beauty standards. These movements advocate for the acceptance and celebration of all body types, promoting the idea that beauty is diverse and inclusive. Body positivity encourages individuals to appreciate their bodies for what they can do rather than how they look, fostering a sense of self-love and acceptance. Social media has played a significant role in amplifying body positivity messages, providing a platform for individuals to share their stories and challenge conventional beauty norms.

However, the body positivity movement is not without its criticisms. Some argue that it can be co-opted by commercial interests, turning a movement aimed at inclusivity into a marketing strategy. Additionally, there is a concern that body positivity may inadvertently shame those who still wish to change their bodies or who do not feel positive about their appearance. A more nuanced approach, often referred to as body neutrality, emphasizes accepting one's body without the pressure to feel positively about it at all times. This perspective focuses on respecting and caring for the body, regardless of how one feels about its appearance.

Addressing body image issues requires a multifaceted approach that involves individuals, families, communities, and society at large. Education and awareness are critical in helping individuals develop a healthy and realistic understanding of body image. Programs that promote media literacy can empower people to critically analyze the messages they receive and recognize the unrealistic standards often portrayed in the media. Encouraging open conversations about body image and mental health can reduce stigma and provide support for those struggling with these issues.

Healthcare professionals, including doctors, therapists, and dietitians, play a crucial role in addressing body image concerns and related mental health issues. Providing comprehensive care that addresses both physical and psychological aspects is essential for supporting individuals with body image issues. Interventions such as cognitive-behavioral therapy (CBT) have been effective in treating body image disturbances and related conditions like eating disorders. These therapies help individuals challenge negative thought patterns, develop healthier coping mechanisms, and build a more positive self-image.

Schools and educational institutions can also contribute to fostering a healthy body image by creating supportive environments and implementing programs that promote self-esteem and body acceptance. Initiatives that encourage physical activity for enjoyment rather than appearance, emphasize the importance of nutrition and wellness over dieting, and celebrate diversity can help students develop a balanced and positive relationship with their bodies.

Chapter 16: Social Media: The Digital Self

Social media has transformed the way we communicate, interact, and present ourselves to the world. The concept of the "digital self" has emerged as individuals curate and construct their identities online, often crafting a version of themselves that may differ significantly from their offline persona. This phenomenon has profound implications for self-perception, social interactions, and mental health.

The digital self is the persona that individuals create and project on social media platforms such as Facebook, Instagram, Twitter, Snapchat, and TikTok. This online identity is often a carefully curated version of oneself, showcasing selected aspects of one's life, personality, and achievements. The construction of the digital self involves choosing what to share, how to present it, and managing the feedback received from others. This process of self-presentation is influenced by various factors, including the desire for social validation, the need to conform to societal norms, and the platform's specific culture and features.

One of the defining characteristics of the digital self is its curated nature. Unlike face-to-face interactions, where spontaneous and unfiltered expressions occur, social media allows individuals to meticulously select the content they share. This selective sharing often highlights positive experiences, achievements, and aspects of life that align with societal ideals of success and happiness. As a result, the digital self can appear more polished, exciting, and attractive than one's offline reality. This curated portrayal can lead to a disconnect between the digital self and the authentic self, creating a sense of pressure to maintain this idealized image.

The pursuit of social validation is a significant driving force behind the construction of the digital self. Social media platforms are designed to facilitate and amplify feedback mechanisms, such as likes, comments, shares, and followers. These metrics serve as indicators of social approval and can significantly influence how individuals feel about themselves. The desire for validation can lead individuals to post content that they believe will garner positive reactions, reinforcing certain behaviors and self-presentation styles. Over time, the need for validation can become addictive, with individuals constantly seeking the next "hit" of social approval to boost their self-esteem.

Social comparison is another critical aspect of the digital self. Social media provides a platform for constant comparison with others, whether they are friends, acquaintances, or celebrities. This comparison is often based on the curated and idealized versions of others' lives, which can create unrealistic standards and expectations. When individuals compare their own lives to these idealized portrayals, they may feel inadequate or envious, leading to negative self-perceptions and reduced self-esteem. The phenomenon of "fear of missing out" (FOMO) exacerbates these feelings, as individuals perceive that others are having more fulfilling and exciting experiences.

The influence of social media on body image is a well-documented example of the impact of the digital self. Platforms like Instagram and TikTok, which emphasize visual content, often promote specific beauty standards and body ideals. The prevalence of edited and filtered images can distort perceptions of reality, making it challenging for individuals to accept their natural appearance. This pressure to conform to digital beauty standards can lead to body dissatisfaction, eating disorders, and other mental health issues. The digital self, in this context, becomes a vehicle for striving towards an unattainable ideal, often at the expense of one's well-being.

The concept of the digital self also extends to identity exploration and experimentation. Social media provides a space where individuals can explore different aspects of their identity, including gender, sexuality, and cultural affiliation. This exploration can be empowering, offering a sense of community and validation that may be lacking in offline environments. For marginalized groups, social media can serve as a platform for self-expression and activism, amplifying voices that might otherwise be silenced. The ability to connect with like-minded individuals and communities can foster a sense of belonging and support.

However, the flexibility of the digital self can also lead to challenges related to authenticity and identity coherence. The ease with which individuals can adopt different personas online can create confusion about one's true self. The pressure to maintain multiple versions of oneself, tailored to different audiences or platforms, can be exhausting and lead to a fragmented sense of identity. Balancing the desire for self-expression with the need for social acceptance can create internal conflicts and stress.

The impact of the digital self on mental health is a growing area of concern and research. The constant exposure to curated content, social comparison, and the pursuit of validation can contribute to anxiety, depression, and other mental health issues. The need to present a flawless digital self can lead to perfectionism and fear of judgment, exacerbating feelings of inadequacy and stress. Social media use has also been linked to sleep disturbances, as individuals spend excessive time online, particularly before bedtime, which can affect overall well-being.

Despite these challenges, social media also offers opportunities for positive self-presentation and personal growth. The digital self can be a platform for showcasing talents, sharing achievements, and building a personal brand. For entrepreneurs, artists, and influencers, social media can be a powerful tool for reaching a broader audience and achieving professional success. The ability to share one's passions and connect with others who share similar interests can foster a sense of fulfillment and purpose.

The rise of influencers and micro-celebrities on social media highlights the potential for the digital self to become a source of income and career advancement. Influencers curate their digital selves to attract followers, secure brand partnerships, and monetize their online presence. This phenomenon has transformed social media from a platform for personal expression to a space for professional opportunities. However, the pressure to constantly produce engaging content and maintain an appealing digital self can also lead to burnout and mental health challenges for influencers.

Social media platforms themselves play a crucial role in shaping the digital self. The algorithms that determine what content is seen and promoted can influence user behavior and self-presentation. Features such as filters, editing tools, and live streaming capabilities provide users with the means to enhance their digital self and engage with their audience. However, these same features can also contribute to the pressure to present an idealized version of oneself and the challenges of maintaining authenticity.

Addressing the complexities of the digital self requires a multifaceted approach that involves individuals, families, educators, and social media companies. Media literacy education can empower individuals to critically analyze the content they consume and understand the mechanics behind social media platforms. Teaching young people about the curated nature of the digital self and the impact of social comparison can help them develop healthier relationships with social media.

Families play a vital role in supporting healthy social media use and fostering open communication about online experiences. Encouraging discussions about the differences between online and offline selves, setting boundaries around social media use, and promoting offline activities can help mitigate the negative effects of social media. Parents and caregivers should model healthy social media behavior and provide guidance on navigating the digital landscape.

Social media companies have a responsibility to create platforms that support the well-being of their users. Implementing features that promote positive interactions, reduce harmful content, and provide resources for mental health support can make a significant difference. Transparency about algorithms and data use, as well as efforts to reduce the prevalence of edited and unrealistic images, can contribute to a healthier online environment.

On an individual level, cultivating self-awareness and mindfulness around social media use is essential. Setting limits on screen time, curating one's feed to include diverse and positive content, and taking breaks from social media can help maintain a balanced perspective. Practicing self-compassion and focusing on self-worth beyond social media validation can strengthen one's sense of identity and resilience.

Chapter 17: Rebellion: Defying Authority

Rebellion, the act of defying authority or societal norms, is a complex and multifaceted phenomenon that has been observed throughout history and across cultures. It represents a fundamental aspect of human behavior, driven by a variety of factors including individualism, social injustice, cultural change, and the quest for autonomy. Rebellion can manifest in various forms, from peaceful protests and civil disobedience to more radical and confrontational actions, each reflecting different motivations and contexts.

At its core, rebellion is often a response to perceived injustice or oppression. Individuals or groups may rebel against authority figures, institutions, or societal norms that they view as unjust, oppressive, or restrictive of their freedoms. This can include political regimes, social hierarchies, cultural traditions, or even parental or institutional rules. Rebellion serves as a means of expressing dissatisfaction, asserting autonomy, and advocating for change.

One of the most notable forms of rebellion is political rebellion, where individuals or groups challenge governmental authority or policies they deem unfair or illegitimate. This can take the form of protests, demonstrations, strikes, or acts of civil disobedience aimed at disrupting the status quo and demanding political reform or revolution. Historical examples abound, such as the American Revolution against British colonial rule, the Civil Rights Movement in the United States, and the Arab Spring protests across the Middle East and North Africa.

Social rebellion, on the other hand, focuses on challenging societal norms and cultural expectations. It often addresses issues related to identity, gender roles, sexuality, and racial equality. Movements advocating for women's rights, LGBTQ+ rights, and racial justice have utilized rebellion as a tool to challenge systemic discrimination and advocate for equal rights and representation. These movements seek to dismantle oppressive structures and create more inclusive and equitable societies.

Cultural rebellion involves challenging established cultural norms, traditions, and artistic conventions. Artists, musicians, writers, and intellectuals often engage in cultural rebellion by creating provocative or subversive works that challenge mainstream values and beliefs. The punk rock movement of the 1970s, for example, rejected the commercialism and conformity of mainstream music, advocating for individualism, anti-establishment values, and DIY ethics. Similarly, avant-garde artists throughout history have pushed the boundaries of artistic expression, challenging conventional aesthetics and societal expectations.

Rebellion can also be personal and internal, reflecting an individual's quest for autonomy and self-expression. Adolescence is a developmental period often characterized by rebellion against parental authority and societal expectations. Teenagers may engage in behaviors such as defiance, experimentation with identity, and questioning of established norms as they navigate the process of self-discovery and autonomy. This form of rebellion is a natural part of identity formation and differentiation from parental influence.

Psychologically, rebellion can serve several functions for individuals and communities. It can provide a sense of empowerment and agency, allowing individuals to assert their values and beliefs in the face of perceived injustice or oppression. Rebellion can foster solidarity among like-minded individuals, creating collective identities and social movements united by a common cause. It can also serve as a catalyst for social change, prompting dialogue, raising awareness, and influencing public opinion and policy.

However, rebellion is not without risks and challenges. Acts of rebellion can provoke resistance, repression, and backlash from authorities or societal institutions seeking to maintain control and stability. Participants in rebellious movements may face consequences such as legal repercussions, social stigma, violence, or marginalization. The success or failure of rebellion often hinges on strategic planning, organizational cohesion, public support, and the ability to sustain momentum over time.

The concept of rebellion raises questions about the balance between individual rights and social order, as well as the ethics of disobedience and resistance. Philosophers and thinkers throughout history have debated the moral justifications for rebellion, exploring concepts such as civil disobedience, moral obligation, and the legitimacy of challenging authority in pursuit of justice or freedom. Figures like Mahatma Gandhi, Martin Luther King Jr., and Nelson Mandela are celebrated for their advocacy of nonviolent resistance and moral leadership in the face of oppression.

In contemporary society, rebellion continues to shape political discourse, social movements, and cultural expressions. The advent of digital technology and social media has democratized activism, enabling individuals to mobilize and amplify their voices on a global scale. Movements such as #BlackLivesMatter, #MeToo, and climate activism have utilized social media platforms to organize protests, raise awareness, and challenge systemic injustices.

The portrayal of rebellion in popular culture often romanticizes acts of defiance and resistance, portraying rebels as heroic figures challenging corrupt or tyrannical authorities. Literature, film, and music frequently explore themes of rebellion, offering narratives that resonate with audiences seeking empowerment, justice, and social change. These cultural representations can inspire individuals to question authority, challenge injustice, and envision a more equitable and inclusive society.

Chapter 18: Mentorship: Guidance from Unexpected Places

Mentorship often evokes images of structured programs and formal relationships, but the most impactful guidance can sometimes come from unexpected places. These unanticipated mentors shape our journey in ways that are subtle yet profound, revealing the immense value of diverse influences in personal development. From childhood through adulthood, mentorship can emerge from various corners of our lives, each offering unique perspectives and lessons that contribute to our growth and understanding of ourselves.

In early childhood, parents and close family members typically serve as the primary mentors, providing foundational lessons in behavior, values, and social norms. These early interactions shape our understanding of the world and our place within it. Parents, through their actions and words, instill confidence and teach us how to navigate the complexities of human relationships. Their guidance is often deliberate, aimed at fostering a sense of security and self-worth. However, children also learn from observing their parents' responses to challenges, conflicts, and successes, absorbing these lessons in ways that might not be immediately apparent.

As children grow and start school, teachers become significant figures in their lives. Teachers, often seen as traditional mentors, provide academic instruction and also model problem-solving, perseverance, and curiosity. They encourage students to explore their interests and expand their horizons, helping them build a foundation of knowledge and critical thinking skills. The influence of a dedicated teacher can ignite a lifelong passion for learning and set the stage for future success. However, it's not only the standout teachers who leave an impact. Sometimes, it's a fleeting comment or a brief interaction that resonates deeply, providing clarity or motivation when it's needed most.

Peers also play a crucial role in mentorship, albeit in less formal ways. Friends offer support, companionship, and a different perspective on shared experiences. Peer mentorship is often reciprocal, with individuals learning from each other's strengths and weaknesses. These relationships teach us about collaboration, empathy, and resilience. The challenges and conflicts that arise within peer groups also provide valuable lessons in negotiation, forgiveness, and understanding. Through these interactions, we learn to navigate the complexities of human emotions and develop a deeper sense of self-awareness.

As we transition into adulthood, the sources of mentorship diversify further. In the workplace, colleagues and supervisors can become mentors, offering guidance on professional development and career advancement. These relationships often develop organically, built on mutual respect and shared goals. A supportive mentor in the workplace can help navigate the intricacies of corporate culture, provide constructive feedback, and open doors to new opportunities. The mentorship from a seasoned professional can accelerate personal growth, helping one to avoid common pitfalls and capitalize on strengths.

Unexpected mentors often appear in everyday life, outside of structured environments. A conversation with a stranger, a chance encounter with someone at a community event, or even an online interaction can provide insights that alter our perspective. These mentors offer fresh viewpoints, challenging our assumptions and encouraging us to think differently. Their guidance is not sought but happens serendipitously, often when we are most receptive to new ideas. These moments of mentorship remind us that learning and growth can occur anywhere and at any time, often when we least expect it.

Moreover, mentorship can also come from unlikely sources such as fictional characters in books, movies, or television shows. Stories have a powerful way of conveying life lessons and moral dilemmas, allowing us to see the world through different lenses. A character's journey can mirror our own struggles and triumphs, providing comfort, inspiration, and guidance. The lessons learned from these fictional mentors can be just as impactful as those from real-life mentors, offering valuable insights into human nature and personal growth.

Mentorship from unexpected places also includes learning from nature and the environment. Observing the resilience of a tree in a storm or the persistence of a river carving its way through rock can teach us about patience, strength, and the importance of adaptability. These natural mentors remind us of the interconnectedness of life and the value of perseverance. They offer lessons in mindfulness and presence, encouraging us to find balance and harmony within ourselves and our surroundings.

In addition to external mentors, self-mentorship is an essential aspect of personal growth. Reflecting on past experiences, setting goals, and seeking out new knowledge are ways we can mentor ourselves. This internal guidance helps us to stay true to our values and continuously strive for improvement. Self-mentorship requires honesty, discipline, and a willingness to learn from both successes and failures. By cultivating self-awareness and a growth mindset, we can become our own best mentors, guiding ourselves through life's challenges with confidence and resilience.

Chapter 19: Discovering Passions: Hobbies and Talents

Discovering passions, whether through hobbies or innate talents, is a deeply enriching journey that profoundly shapes our identities and personal fulfillment. This exploration often begins in childhood, a time of curiosity and boundless energy, where every new activity is an opportunity for discovery. Parents and guardians play a crucial role in this phase, introducing children to a variety of activities such as sports, music, arts, and academics. These early experiences can plant the seeds of lifelong passions, as children experiment with different pursuits to find what resonates with them.

Children's innate curiosity and lack of preconceived notions about success or failure allow them to explore freely, often leading to the discovery of surprising talents. For example, a child given a paintbrush might uncover a remarkable aptitude for art, or one who picks up a musical instrument could demonstrate a natural ear for music. These early signs of talent can be nurtured through encouragement and resources, enabling the child to develop their skills and passion further. The joy and satisfaction derived from these activities provide positive reinforcement, fostering a love for the activity that can last a lifetime.

As individuals grow older, their hobbies and interests often evolve. Adolescence is a particularly critical period for discovering passions, as teenagers seek to establish their identities and independence. This is a time when school clubs, extracurricular activities, and social groups can play a significant role. Participating in a variety of activities allows teenagers to explore different facets of their personalities and interests. Peer influence also becomes more pronounced, with friends often introducing each other to new hobbies and interests. The support and camaraderie of friends can encourage teenagers to pursue their passions more seriously and with greater confidence.

In addition to structured activities, informal exploration is equally important. Casual hobbies like reading, hiking, cooking, or gaming can reveal unexpected talents and interests. The digital age has vastly expanded the range of accessible hobbies, with online platforms providing tutorials and communities for virtually any interest. Whether it's learning to code, joining an online book club, or following fitness tutorials, the internet offers a wealth of resources for discovering and nurturing passions. The ability to connect with like-minded individuals globally also creates a sense of belonging and motivation, further fueling one's passion.

Adulthood often brings new responsibilities and constraints, but it also offers greater autonomy in pursuing passions. Many adults rediscover hobbies they enjoyed in their youth or take up new ones inspired by different life experiences. The workplace, too, can be a source of passion discovery, as career roles often align with personal interests and skills. For example, someone with a passion for helping others might find fulfillment in a career in healthcare or social work. Similarly, those with a knack for problem-solving might thrive in fields like engineering or software development. Professional success and personal satisfaction often intersect when careers are aligned with passions, leading to a more fulfilling life.

However, discovering passions is not always a straightforward path. Many people face challenges such as limited resources, time constraints, or lack of support, which can hinder the exploration of hobbies and talents. Overcoming these obstacles often requires creativity and determination. Finding small pockets of time, seeking out affordable resources, and building a supportive network are crucial steps. Moreover, the pursuit of passion should not be seen as a luxury but as an integral part of well-being and personal growth. Engaging in activities that bring joy and fulfillment can significantly enhance mental and emotional health, providing a necessary balance to the demands of daily life.

For some, the journey to discovering passions may involve trial and error. It's not uncommon to try several hobbies before finding one that truly resonates. This process requires an open mind and a willingness to step out of one's comfort zone. It's important to approach new activities without the fear of failure, viewing each experience as a learning opportunity. The insights gained from exploring different hobbies can lead to a deeper understanding of oneself and one's preferences. Even activities that don't become long-term passions can contribute to personal growth and broaden one's perspective.

Mentorship and community play a significant role in nurturing hobbies and talents. Connecting with others who share similar interests can provide valuable guidance, support, and motivation. Mentors, whether formal or informal, can offer insights and advice based on their own experiences, helping individuals to navigate challenges and set achievable goals. Community groups and clubs offer a sense of belonging and can be a source of inspiration, pushing individuals to improve and strive for excellence. The collective experience of a group can also open up new avenues for exploration, introducing members to related interests and activities.

The discovery of passions is not static; it evolves throughout one's life. As people grow and their circumstances change, so too do their interests and capabilities. A hobby taken up in retirement might be very different from one pursued in youth, yet both can be equally fulfilling. This lifelong journey underscores the importance of remaining open to new experiences and continually seeking out activities that bring joy and satisfaction. The flexibility to adapt and explore new interests ensures that life remains rich and vibrant, regardless of age or stage.

Chapter 20: Self-Expression: Finding My Voice

Self-expression is a fundamental aspect of human existence, deeply intertwined with the journey of finding one's voice. This journey is a lifelong process that begins in early childhood and continues through various stages of life, shaped by personal experiences, cultural influences, and the evolving sense of identity. Finding one's voice is not merely about developing the ability to articulate thoughts and feelings, but also about discovering and embracing the unique ways in which we present ourselves to the world. It involves understanding and asserting our individuality, creativity, and values, while navigating the complexities of social expectations and personal aspirations.

In the early years of life, self-expression is often encouraged through play and creative activities. Children naturally experiment with different forms of expression, such as drawing, singing, storytelling, and role-playing. These activities allow them to explore their imagination and communicate their inner world. Parents and caregivers play a crucial role in this stage by providing a supportive environment that fosters creativity and self-discovery. Encouragement and positive reinforcement help children to build confidence in their abilities and to understand that their thoughts and feelings are valued. This early foundation is essential for developing a sense of self-worth and the courage to express oneself authentically.

As children enter school, the range of opportunities for self-expression expands. Education systems that emphasize holistic development recognize the importance of arts, music, drama, and sports in nurturing students' expressive capabilities. Teachers can inspire and guide students to find their voice by encouraging them to participate in various activities, share their ideas, and collaborate with peers. The school environment also introduces children to a broader spectrum of social interactions, which can influence their self-expression. Peer relationships play a significant role in shaping how children perceive themselves and their willingness to express their individuality. Positive peer interactions can boost self-esteem and encourage open expression, while negative experiences can sometimes lead to self-doubt and reticence.

Adolescence is a particularly transformative period for self-expression. During this time, individuals grapple with questions of identity, belonging, and self-worth. Teenagers often explore different personas and interests as they seek to define who they are. This exploration is a crucial part of finding one's voice. Adolescents may turn to various forms of self-expression, such as fashion, music, writing, or activism, to articulate their evolving identities and connect with others who share similar values and interests. Social media and digital platforms have become significant outlets for self-expression, allowing teenagers to share their thoughts, creativity, and experiences with a wider audience. However, the digital age also brings challenges, such as the pressure to conform to online trends and the impact of negative feedback, which can affect an individual's confidence and authenticity.

As individuals transition into adulthood, the quest for self-expression continues to evolve. Adult life presents new opportunities and challenges that shape how people express themselves. Career choices, relationships, and personal aspirations all influence one's voice. Finding a career that aligns with one's passions and values can be a powerful form of self-expression, allowing individuals to contribute meaningfully to their fields and society. Professional environments can either foster or hinder self-expression, depending on the culture and leadership within an organization. Supportive workplaces that value diversity and creativity enable individuals to bring their authentic selves to their roles, enhancing job satisfaction and productivity.

Personal relationships are another crucial area where self-expression plays a vital role. Effective communication is key to building and maintaining healthy relationships. Being able to express one's thoughts, feelings, and needs openly and honestly is essential for mutual understanding and emotional connection. Relationships that encourage authenticity and mutual respect provide a safe space for individuals to express themselves without fear of judgment or rejection. Conversely, relationships characterized by control or criticism can stifle self-expression and lead to feelings of isolation and inadequacy.

Creativity remains a significant outlet for self-expression throughout adulthood. Engaging in creative activities, whether as a hobby or a profession, allows individuals to explore their inner world and communicate their unique perspectives. Writing, painting, music, dance, and other forms of artistic expression provide a means to process emotions, reflect on experiences, and share one's story. The creative process itself can be a journey of self-discovery, revealing insights about one's values, desires, and strengths. Many adults find that returning to creative pursuits, either those they enjoyed in youth or new interests discovered later in life, brings a renewed sense of purpose and fulfillment.

Self-expression is also closely linked to cultural identity and heritage. Understanding and embracing one's cultural background can enrich self-expression by providing a deeper sense of belonging and connection to a larger community. Cultural traditions, languages, and practices offer unique ways of expressing oneself and honoring one's heritage. At the same time, individuals may also navigate the complexities of integrating multiple cultural identities, particularly in multicultural societies. This can lead to a rich tapestry of self-expression that draws from diverse influences and experiences.

Finding one's voice is not a linear process; it involves ongoing reflection, adaptation, and growth. Life events, such as significant achievements, losses, or transitions, can prompt individuals to reassess and redefine their self-expression. Personal growth often involves overcoming fears and insecurities that inhibit authentic expression. Developing self-awareness and emotional intelligence helps individuals to understand their motivations and barriers to self-expression. Practices such as mindfulness, journaling, and therapy can facilitate this introspective journey, enabling individuals to articulate their thoughts and feelings more clearly and confidently.

Moreover, the journey of finding one's voice is deeply interconnected with the broader social and political context. Societal norms, power dynamics, and issues of equity and justice influence how individuals express themselves and whose voices are heard. Advocacy and activism can be powerful forms of self-expression, allowing individuals to stand up for their beliefs and contribute to social change. Through activism, people can find a collective voice that amplifies their impact and fosters a sense of solidarity with others who share their cause.

Chapter 21: Leaving Home: The Road to Independence

Leaving home and embarking on the road to independence is a significant milestone in a person's life, representing a crucial transition from the familiar comforts and guidance of family life to the broader, often challenging landscape of self-sufficiency. This journey is complex and multifaceted, involving emotional, psychological, financial, and social adjustments. The process varies widely among individuals, shaped by cultural backgrounds, personal circumstances, and the socio-economic environment, yet it universally marks a pivotal moment of growth and self-discovery.

The initial decision to leave home is often driven by various factors, including the pursuit of higher education, employment opportunities, personal growth, or a desire for autonomy. For many, the journey begins with attending college or university. This step not only signifies a move towards academic and professional development but also necessitates adapting to new social environments and living independently. College life often provides a structured yet liberating environment where individuals can explore their identities, forge new relationships, and develop essential life skills. The dormitory experience, sharing spaces with peers from diverse backgrounds, and managing daily responsibilities without direct parental oversight are all part of this formative phase.

For others, the path to independence might be through entering the workforce directly after high school. This transition can be both exciting and daunting, as it involves securing employment, managing finances, and often living alone or with roommates for the first time. The workforce introduces young adults to the realities of job responsibilities, workplace dynamics, and the importance of financial planning. Managing rent, utilities, groceries, and other expenses requires a level of financial literacy and discipline that is new to many. Learning to balance work demands with personal life is another critical aspect of this stage, contributing to the development of time management and organizational skills.

Leaving home also encompasses the emotional journey of separating from the familial unit. This transition can evoke a mix of emotions, including excitement, anxiety, loneliness, and liberation. The sense of leaving behind a familiar support system and stepping into the unknown requires emotional resilience. Maintaining relationships with family while establishing independence is a delicate balance. Regular communication, visits, and maintaining traditions can help mitigate feelings of homesickness and strengthen familial bonds, even from a distance. The support of family and friends remains crucial during this period, providing a safety net while encouraging the growth of independence.

The road to independence also involves significant psychological adjustments. The newfound freedom to make decisions can be both empowering and overwhelming. Young adults must navigate a myriad of choices regarding their lifestyle, career path, social circles, and personal values. This decision-making process is a critical component of developing self-efficacy and confidence. Experiencing successes and setbacks in this phase contributes to building resilience and adaptability. It is through these experiences that individuals learn to trust their judgment, handle uncertainty, and take responsibility for their actions.

The financial aspect of leaving home cannot be understated. Financial independence is a cornerstone of overall autonomy. Managing finances effectively is a skill that often requires learning through experience. Budgeting, saving, investing, and understanding credit are essential components of financial literacy. The reality of financial constraints can be a harsh adjustment, but it also instills a sense of discipline and foresight. Many young adults might take on part-time jobs, internships, or freelance work to support themselves while pursuing further education or early in their careers. These experiences not only provide financial support but also enhance professional skills and work ethic.

Living independently also means taking on household responsibilities. Cooking, cleaning, maintaining a living space, and managing time effectively are practical skills that contribute to overall independence. These tasks, while seemingly mundane, are integral to sustaining a healthy and organized life. Learning to cook nutritious meals, keep a clean-living environment, and manage personal time efficiently are all part of developing a balanced lifestyle. These skills foster self-reliance and contribute to a sense of accomplishment and personal competence.

Social relationships undergo significant changes during the transition to independence. Leaving the familiar social circles of home and school to build new relationships in a new environment requires social skills and emotional intelligence. Forming connections with colleagues, classmates, and neighbors creates a new support network. These relationships can be instrumental in personal and professional growth, providing opportunities for mentorship, collaboration, and mutual support. Navigating social dynamics, building friendships, and establishing boundaries are all part of the social learning that accompanies independence.

The journey to independence also involves exploring and understanding one's identity. The freedom to make choices about one's lifestyle, career, and social interactions provides the opportunity to explore personal values, beliefs, and aspirations. This self-exploration is a vital part of personal growth, leading to a deeper understanding of one's strengths, weaknesses, and passions. The process of self-discovery often involves experimentation, reflection, and sometimes, re-evaluation of long-held beliefs. This period of exploration can be empowering, allowing individuals to align their lives more closely with their true selves and long-term goals.

Cultural background significantly influences the experience of leaving home. In some cultures, there is a strong emphasis on family cohesion and interdependence, and leaving home might occur later or involve different dynamics compared to cultures that prioritize individualism and early independence. Understanding and respecting cultural differences in the transition to independence is important. In some cases, individuals might find themselves navigating the expectations of their cultural heritage while pursuing their personal path to independence, which can add a layer of complexity to the journey.

Challenges and setbacks are an inevitable part of the road to independence. Facing and overcoming these challenges is crucial for building resilience and problem-solving skills. Whether it is financial difficulties, academic pressures, job stress, or personal conflicts, these experiences teach valuable lessons about perseverance and adaptability. The ability to learn from mistakes, seek help when needed, and continually strive for improvement is a hallmark of a successful transition to independence.

Technology plays a significant role in modern independence. Digital tools and platforms facilitate many aspects of independent living, from managing finances and time to staying connected with family and friends. Online resources provide access to information and services that support self-sufficiency, such as online banking, e-learning, and telehealth services. However, the reliance on technology also requires a level of digital literacy and awareness of cybersecurity and privacy issues.

The journey to independence is not a solitary endeavor; it is supported by a network of relationships and resources. Mentorship, whether from family, educators, employers, or peers, provides guidance and support. Access to educational and career opportunities, mental health resources, and community services also plays a critical role in facilitating a successful transition. The ability to seek out and utilize these resources effectively is a skill that enhances overall independence.

89

Chapter 22: College Life: New Beginnings

College life represents a profound new beginning, marking the transition from adolescence to adulthood. This period is characterized by a series of transformative experiences that encompass academic growth, personal development, social interactions, and the exploration of newfound independence. College is not merely a continuation of formal education; it is a unique phase that shapes an individual's identity, values, and future trajectory in profound ways.

From the moment students step onto a college campus, they are thrust into an environment that challenges them to think critically, manage their time effectively, and navigate a multitude of social dynamics. This transition begins with orientation programs designed to acclimate new students to college life. These programs introduce students to the campus layout, academic expectations, and available resources. Orientation is often the first opportunity for students to meet their peers, establish initial connections, and begin forming friendships that may last a lifetime. This initial period can be both exhilarating and overwhelming as students adjust to living away from home and take on new responsibilities.

Academically, college represents a significant shift from the structured environment of high school to a more self-directed form of learning. Students are expected to take greater ownership of their education, from selecting courses that align with their interests and career aspirations to managing their study schedules. The diversity of courses available in college allows students to explore different fields of knowledge, often leading to the discovery of new passions and interests. The flexibility to choose majors, minors, and electives enables students to tailor their academic journey to their unique goals and aspirations.

College professors play a crucial role in this academic journey. Unlike high school teachers, who often provide more guided instruction, college professors encourage independent thinking and self-motivation. They serve not only as educators but also as mentors, guiding students through complex subjects and inspiring them to delve deeper into their areas of interest. The opportunity to engage with faculty members through office hours, research projects, and seminars enriches the learning experience and provides valuable insights into various academic and professional fields.

The collegiate environment also fosters the development of critical thinking and problem-solving skills. Through rigorous coursework, research opportunities, and intellectual discussions, students are encouraged to question assumptions, analyze information, and develop well-reasoned arguments. These skills are not only essential for academic success but also for navigating the complexities of life beyond college. Participation in debates, presentations, and group projects further hones communication and collaboration abilities, preparing students for the demands of the professional world.

Outside the classroom, college life offers a wealth of opportunities for personal growth and self-discovery. Extracurricular activities, such as clubs, sports, and volunteer organizations, provide avenues for students to pursue their interests, develop new skills, and build a sense of community. Involvement in these activities enhances leadership, teamwork, and organizational skills. Whether it's joining a debate club, participating in a theater production, or playing on a sports team, these experiences contribute to a well-rounded education and foster a sense of belonging.

Greek life, including fraternities and sororities, is another significant aspect of college life for many students. These organizations offer social, philanthropic, and leadership opportunities, creating tight-knit communities and lifelong friendships. While Greek life can enhance the college experience, it also requires a commitment to balancing academic responsibilities with social activities and community service.

Living on campus is often a defining feature of the college experience. Dormitory life introduces students to a communal living environment, where they share spaces with peers from diverse backgrounds. This exposure to different cultures, perspectives, and lifestyles broadens students' understanding of the world and enhances their interpersonal skills. The challenges of living with roommates, managing conflicts, and maintaining a healthy living environment contribute to personal growth and the development of important life skills.

Financial independence is another critical aspect of college life. Many students manage their finances for the first time, dealing with tuition, housing costs, meal plans, and personal expenses. Budgeting, financial planning, and managing student loans are essential skills that students must develop to navigate the financial realities of college. Part-time jobs, internships, and work-study programs provide not only financial support but also valuable work experience and professional connections.

Mental health and well-being are paramount during the college years. The transition to college, academic pressures, and social dynamics can be stressful. Colleges and universities recognize the importance of supporting students' mental health and offer resources such as counseling services, wellness programs, and stress management workshops. Building a support network of friends, mentors, and mental health professionals is crucial for maintaining emotional well-being.

The diversity of the college community enriches the overall experience. Students from different cultural, ethnic, and socioeconomic backgrounds bring a variety of perspectives and experiences to the campus. This diversity fosters an inclusive environment where students can learn from one another, challenge their preconceptions, and develop a global outlook. Interacting with peers from different backgrounds enhances cultural competency and prepares students for working in an increasingly interconnected world.

Technology plays a significant role in modern college life. Digital tools and platforms facilitate learning, research, and communication. Online learning management systems, virtual libraries, and digital collaboration tools enhance the educational experience and provide flexibility in how students engage with their coursework. Social media and communication apps help students stay connected with friends and family, manage their social lives, and access support networks.

Study abroad programs offer another dimension to college life, providing students with the opportunity to immerse themselves in different cultures, languages, and educational systems. These experiences broaden students' horizons, enhance their global awareness, and often lead to personal and academic growth. The challenges of adapting to a new environment and navigating cultural differences build resilience and adaptability.

The college experience culminates in the development of a strong sense of self and a clearer understanding of one's goals and aspirations. The journey through college is marked by moments of self-reflection, exploration, and discovery. Students learn to navigate challenges, celebrate achievements, and build a foundation for their future careers and personal lives. The friendships formed, the knowledge gained, and the experiences lived during college shape individuals in profound ways, leaving a lasting impact on their identities and trajectories.

Graduation marks the end of the college journey but also the beginning of a new chapter. The transition from college to the professional world brings new challenges and opportunities. The skills, knowledge, and experiences acquired during college provide a strong foundation for navigating the complexities of adult life. Alumni networks, career services, and continued connections with mentors and peers offer support as graduates embark on their professional paths.

94

Chapter 23: Career Choices: Pathways and Pitfalls

Career choices represent a critical juncture in one's life, significantly influencing personal fulfillment, financial stability, and overall life satisfaction. The process of making career choices is multifaceted, involving self-assessment, exploration of options, decision-making, and ongoing adjustments. Each phase of this process presents its own set of pathways and pitfalls that can shape an individual's career trajectory in profound ways. Understanding these elements in detail can help individuals navigate their career journey more effectively and achieve greater satisfaction and success.

The journey of career choice often begins with self-assessment. This initial phase involves a deep exploration of one's interests, values, skills, and personality traits. Tools such as personality assessments (e.g., Myers-Briggs Type Indicator), interest inventories (e.g., Holland Code), and skills assessments can provide valuable insights into potential career paths that align with an individual's intrinsic motivations and strengths. For instance, someone with a strong inclination towards helping others and a high level of empathy might be well-suited for careers in healthcare, social work, or education. On the other hand, an individual with a knack for problem-solving and a passion for technology might thrive in engineering, computer science, or data analysis.

However, self-assessment is not without its pitfalls. It requires honest reflection and sometimes professional guidance to avoid biases and misconceptions about one's abilities and preferences. Overestimating or underestimating one's skills can lead to career choices that are either overly ambitious or insufficiently challenging. Additionally, societal pressures and family expectations can skew self-assessment, leading individuals to pursue paths that do not truly resonate with their personal values and interests.

Following self-assessment, the exploration of career options is the next critical phase. This involves researching various professions, understanding the day-to-day responsibilities, required qualifications, potential for growth, and long-term stability. Job shadowing, internships, informational interviews, and industry conferences are valuable ways to gain firsthand insights into different fields. For example, an internship in a law firm can provide a clear picture of what a legal career entails, helping an individual decide whether to pursue law school.

The exploration phase also includes considering educational pathways. Choosing the right educational institution and program can significantly impact career opportunities. Attending a prestigious university with a strong program in one's chosen field can open doors to high-profile internships and job placements. Moreover, specialized certifications and training programs can enhance employability in specific industries. For instance, obtaining a Project Management Professional (PMP) certification can be highly beneficial for someone interested in a career in project management.

Despite the wealth of information available, the exploration phase has its own set of pitfalls. Relying solely on online research or secondary sources without gaining practical experience can lead to a superficial understanding of a career. Additionally, focusing too narrowly on high-profile or glamorous professions can result in overlooking equally rewarding but less publicized career paths. It is crucial to maintain a broad perspective and consider a range of options before making a final decision.

Decision-making is arguably the most challenging phase of career choice. This involves synthesizing information from self-assessment and exploration to make an informed choice. Several factors come into play during this phase, including personal interests, financial considerations, job market trends, and long-term career goals. Decision-making tools such as pros and cons lists, decision matrices, and career counseling can aid in this process. For instance, a decision matrix can help weigh various factors such as salary, job satisfaction, work-life balance, and advancement opportunities for different career options.

A significant pitfall in the decision-making phase is the fear of making the wrong choice. The pressure to choose a "perfect" career can lead to indecision or paralysis by analysis. It is important to recognize that career choices are not set in stone and that flexibility and adaptability are crucial in today's dynamic job market. Another common pitfall is neglecting the importance of job satisfaction and focusing solely on financial rewards. While a lucrative salary is important, it should not come at the expense of personal fulfillment and well-being.

Once a career choice is made, the next phase involves preparing for and entering the chosen field. This includes obtaining necessary education, gaining relevant experience, and building a professional network. Higher education institutions, vocational schools, and training programs provide the knowledge and credentials needed to enter a particular profession. Practical experience through internships, part-time jobs, and volunteer work is equally important, as it provides hands-on skills and enhances employability.

Networking is a critical aspect of career preparation. Building connections with professionals in the field can lead to job opportunities, mentorship, and valuable industry insights. Attending networking events, joining professional associations, and utilizing platforms like LinkedIn can facilitate these connections. For instance, a student aspiring to work in marketing might benefit from joining the American Marketing Association (AMA) to connect with industry professionals and stay updated on the latest trends and opportunities.

The entry into the job market marks the beginning of one's professional journey. This phase involves applying for jobs, preparing for interviews, and negotiating job offers. Crafting a compelling resume and cover letter that highlight relevant skills and experiences is essential. Interview preparation, including practicing common questions and developing a strong personal pitch, can enhance confidence and performance during job interviews.

However, entering the job market is not without its challenges. Job search can be a time-consuming and sometimes discouraging process, especially in competitive fields. Rejection is a common experience, and it is important to remain resilient and persistent. Additionally, the transition from academic life to professional work can be challenging, requiring adjustments in time management, work habits, and professional demeanor.

Once employed, the focus shifts to career development and progression. This involves continuous learning, performance improvement, and seeking opportunities for advancement. Professional development can take various forms, including on-the-job training, pursuing advanced degrees, obtaining additional certifications, and attending industry conferences and workshops. Staying updated with industry trends and technologies is crucial for maintaining competitiveness in the job market.

Building a positive professional reputation and demonstrating a strong work ethic can lead to promotions and career advancement. Seeking feedback, setting career goals, and proactively taking on challenging projects can enhance career growth. Networking continues to play a vital role, as connections within the industry can lead to new opportunities and collaborations.

Despite careful planning and effort, career paths are rarely linear. Unexpected changes in the job market, personal circumstances, and evolving interests can lead to career shifts and transitions. Embracing flexibility and adaptability is essential for navigating these changes successfully. Career transitions might involve changing industries, pursuing different roles within the same field, or even starting a new business venture. Each transition presents an opportunity for growth and reinvention.

The process of making career choices also involves recognizing and addressing potential pitfalls. One significant pitfall is the influence of external expectations and societal norms. Pressure from family, friends, or societal expectations can lead individuals to pursue careers that do not align with their true interests and values. It is important to stay true to oneself and make career choices based on personal fulfillment rather than external validation.

Another pitfall is the risk of burnout and job dissatisfaction. Pursuing a demanding career without maintaining a healthy work-life balance can lead to physical and mental exhaustion. Prioritizing self-care, setting boundaries, and seeking supportive work environments are essential for long-term career satisfaction and well-being.

Chapter 24: First Job: Entering the Workforce

Entering the workforce for the first time is a pivotal moment in one's life, marking the transition from academic life to the professional world. The first job is often seen as a rite of passage, representing the beginning of financial independence, the application of acquired knowledge, and the start of a career. This phase is filled with a mix of excitement, anxiety, challenges, and opportunities. The journey from securing that first job to navigating the workplace is multifaceted and profoundly impactful on an individual's future professional trajectory and personal development.

Securing the first job begins with an extensive job search process. This involves identifying potential employers, crafting tailored resumes and cover letters, and preparing for interviews. Job search strategies vary, but common methods include utilizing online job portals, attending career fairs, networking, and leveraging social media platforms like LinkedIn. Each application requires careful customization to highlight relevant skills, experiences, and how they align with the job requirements. Crafting a compelling resume that effectively showcases one's qualifications and a cover letter that narrates the story behind those qualifications are crucial steps in this process. Preparing for interviews involves researching the company, understanding the job role, and practicing responses to common interview questions. Mock interviews, either with friends or career counselors, can help build confidence and improve communication skills.

The interview process itself can be both thrilling and nerve-wracking. It is an opportunity to make a strong first impression and demonstrate why one is the ideal candidate for the role. Interviews often consist of behavioral questions, technical assessments, and sometimes, case studies or practical tasks relevant to the job. Behavioral questions are designed to assess how candidates have handled various situations in the past, providing insight into their problem-solving abilities, teamwork, and adaptability. Technical assessments or practical tasks evaluate the candidate's specific skills and knowledge relevant to the job. Successfully navigating the interview process requires a blend of confidence, preparation, and the ability to articulate one's experiences and skills effectively.

Once a job offer is received, the negotiation phase begins. This is an essential yet often daunting aspect for many first-time job seekers. Salary negotiation, benefits, work hours, and other employment terms are discussed during this phase. It is crucial to approach this process with research and preparation, understanding industry standards for the role and being clear about one's own requirements and expectations. Effective negotiation can lead to a more satisfactory employment package and set a positive tone for the employer-employee relationship.

Starting the first job introduces a new set of challenges and learning experiences. The initial period, often referred to as the onboarding process, is critical for acclimatizing to the new work environment. Onboarding typically includes orientation sessions, training programs, and introductions to team members and organizational processes. This phase helps new employees understand the company's culture, values, and expectations. A well-structured onboarding process can significantly enhance a new hire's ability to integrate smoothly into the workplace and start contributing effectively.

Adapting to the workplace culture is a vital aspect of entering the workforce. Each organization has its own unique culture, which encompasses its values, norms, and ways of working. Understanding and aligning with this culture can influence an individual's success and satisfaction in their role. Building relationships with colleagues, participating in team activities, and observing workplace etiquette are essential for fitting into the organizational culture. Effective communication, showing respect for others, and demonstrating a willingness to learn are key behaviors that help in building a positive reputation within the workplace.

The transition from academic life to a structured work routine can be challenging. Adjusting to a fixed schedule, managing workloads, and meeting deadlines require a shift in time management and organizational skills. Unlike academic life, where there might be more flexibility and periods of intense but intermittent work, professional life often demands consistent productivity and adherence to schedules. Developing effective time management strategies, such as prioritizing tasks, setting goals, and using organizational tools like calendars and task lists, is crucial for managing responsibilities efficiently.

The first job also provides an opportunity to apply theoretical knowledge in practical settings. This application often highlights the gap between academic learning and real-world practice. Bridging this gap involves continuous learning and adaptability. New employees must be open to learning from their experiences, seeking feedback, and making improvements. Mentorship and guidance from more experienced colleagues can be invaluable in this learning process. Mentors can provide insights into navigating workplace challenges, understanding the industry, and developing professional skills.

Building professional skills is a continuous process that begins with the first job. Communication skills, both verbal and written, are essential for effective workplace interactions. This includes the ability to articulate ideas clearly, listen actively, and engage in constructive discussions. Technical skills relevant to the job are equally important and may require ongoing training and development. Many organizations offer professional development programs, workshops, and courses to help employees enhance their skills. Taking advantage of these opportunities demonstrates a commitment to growth and can lead to career advancement.

Networking within and outside the organization is another crucial aspect of career development. Building a professional network involves establishing connections with colleagues, industry professionals, and mentors. These connections can provide support, guidance, and opportunities for career advancement. Networking can be facilitated through professional associations, industry conferences, and social events. Engaging in networking activities helps in staying updated with industry trends, gaining new insights, and accessing job opportunities.

Handling workplace challenges effectively is critical for professional growth. Challenges can range from dealing with difficult colleagues and managing workload pressures to navigating organizational changes. Developing problem-solving skills, maintaining a positive attitude, and seeking constructive solutions are essential for overcoming these challenges. Conflict resolution skills are particularly important, as interpersonal conflicts can impact team dynamics and productivity. Approaching conflicts with empathy, active listening, and a focus on finding mutually acceptable solutions can help maintain a harmonious work environment.

Maintaining a healthy work-life balance is another important aspect of entering the workforce. The demands of a new job can sometimes lead to long hours and increased stress. It is essential to establish boundaries and prioritize self-care to avoid burnout. This includes setting aside time for relaxation, hobbies, exercise, and social activities. A balanced approach to work and personal life contributes to overall well-being and sustained productivity.

The financial independence gained from the first job is both empowering and challenging. Managing finances responsibly is crucial for achieving long-term financial stability. This includes budgeting, saving, and planning for future financial goals. Understanding and utilizing employee benefits, such as retirement plans, health insurance, and other perks, can enhance financial security. Seeking advice from financial planners or using financial management tools can help in making informed financial decisions.

As the first job progresses, it is important to set career goals and work towards achieving them. Setting short-term and long-term goals provides direction and motivation. Regularly reviewing and adjusting these goals in response to changing circumstances and aspirations is essential for continuous career development. Seeking feedback from supervisors, engaging in self-assessment, and taking on new challenges contribute to professional growth and achievement of career objectives.

The first job also provides a foundation for future career transitions. The experiences, skills, and networks developed during this period can open doors to new opportunities. Being proactive in seeking new challenges, continuously learning, and maintaining a positive professional reputation are key to career advancement. Transitioning to new roles, whether within the same organization or in a different company, often involves leveraging the experience and skills gained in the first job.

Chapter 25: Friendships in Adulthood

Friendships in adulthood differ significantly from those formed during childhood or adolescence. They often reflect deeper connections, mutual respect, and shared life experiences. As people mature, they tend to value the quality of their friendships over the quantity. This shift is influenced by various factors, including personal growth, changing priorities, and the complexities of adult life. Understanding the dynamics of adult friendships involves examining how they form, evolve, and impact one's well-being.

Adult friendships often begin through shared activities, interests, or life stages. Unlike childhood, where proximity (such as living in the same neighborhood or attending the same school) often dictated friendships, adult relationships frequently develop in more selective environments. This can include the workplace, community organizations, hobbies, or through mutual friends. These settings provide opportunities for individuals to connect with others who share similar values, goals, and interests.

As adults navigate their careers, relationships, and personal goals, the time available for social interactions becomes limited. This scarcity of time necessitates a more selective approach to friendships. Adults tend to prioritize relationships that are mutually fulfilling and supportive. The concept of quality over quantity becomes particularly relevant as maintaining numerous superficial friendships can be draining and unsustainable. Instead, investing in a few meaningful relationships can provide greater emotional and psychological benefits.

The nature of adult friendships is often characterized by emotional depth and resilience. These relationships are built on mutual understanding, respect, and a willingness to support one another through various life challenges. Whether it's dealing with career stress, family issues, or personal struggles, having friends who provide a safe space for open and honest communication is invaluable. Such friendships offer not only companionship but also a sense of security and trust.

Trust is a cornerstone of adult friendships. Trusting friends with personal thoughts, fears, and aspirations fosters a deeper connection. This trust is earned over time through consistent behavior, reliability, and emotional support. It is this mutual trust that often distinguishes quality friendships from casual acquaintances. When trust is reciprocated, it strengthens the bond, making the friendship more resilient to conflicts and misunderstandings.

Emotional support is another critical aspect of adult friendships. Life's complexities and pressures can be overwhelming, and having friends who offer empathy, encouragement, and a listening ear can significantly improve one's mental health. This emotional support can manifest in various ways, from providing a shoulder to cry on during tough times to celebrating successes and milestones. The presence of emotionally supportive friends can reduce feelings of loneliness and isolation, contributing to overall well-being.

Reciprocity is fundamental to maintaining adult friendships. Unlike childhood friendships, which can sometimes be one-sided, adult relationships thrive on a balanced give-and-take. This reciprocity involves not only emotional support but also practical help and shared experiences. Whether it's helping a friend move, offering career advice, or simply spending quality time together, reciprocal actions strengthen the friendship and ensure that both parties feel valued and appreciated.

The evolution of adult friendships is often influenced by significant life changes such as marriage, parenthood, career shifts, or relocation. These transitions can strain existing friendships but also offer opportunities to form new ones. For instance, becoming a parent can lead to connections with other parents who share similar experiences and challenges. While some friendships may fade due to changing circumstances, those that endure often become more robust and meaningful.

Technology and social media have transformed how adults maintain and nurture friendships. While face-to-face interactions remain vital, digital communication allows friends to stay connected despite geographical distances. Social media platforms, messaging apps, and video calls facilitate regular communication, enabling friends to share their lives and support each other regardless of physical proximity. However, it's essential to balance online interactions with in-person connections to maintain the depth and authenticity of the friendship.

Balancing work, family, and friendships is a common challenge for adults. The demands of a career and personal responsibilities can limit the time and energy available for social interactions. Prioritizing friendships requires intentional effort and time management. Scheduling regular catch-ups, making time for social activities, and being present in the moment can help maintain strong connections. It's about finding a balance that allows for the cultivation of meaningful relationships without compromising other important aspects of life.

Boundaries play a crucial role in adult friendships. Healthy boundaries ensure that both individuals' needs and limits are respected. This can involve setting expectations around communication, time spent together, and the level of support provided. Clear boundaries help prevent misunderstandings and ensure that the friendship remains mutually beneficial. Respecting each other's boundaries fosters trust and prevents potential conflicts from escalating.

Conflict resolution is an inevitable part of maintaining adult friendships. Disagreements and misunderstandings can arise, but how they are handled determines the strength and longevity of the relationship. Open communication, empathy, and a willingness to listen are essential for resolving conflicts. Addressing issues directly and respectfully allows friends to understand each other's perspectives and find common ground. Effective conflict resolution can strengthen the friendship by demonstrating commitment and mutual respect.

Shared values and goals often underpin the strongest adult friendships. While differences in interests and opinions can enrich a friendship, having core values and long-term goals in common creates a solid foundation. These shared values can include similar attitudes towards work, family, and personal growth. When friends are aligned in their values, it fosters a deeper understanding and connection.

The impact of adult friendships on mental health cannot be overstated. High-quality friendships provide emotional support, reduce stress, and enhance overall life satisfaction. Engaging in meaningful conversations, sharing laughter, and participating in enjoyable activities with friends contribute to a positive outlook and emotional resilience. Conversely, the absence of supportive friendships can lead to feelings of loneliness, depression, and decreased life satisfaction.

Friendships in adulthood also offer opportunities for personal growth and self-discovery. Friends can provide honest feedback, challenge each other's perspectives, and inspire personal development. Engaging with friends who have different experiences and viewpoints broadens one's horizons and fosters intellectual and emotional growth. These interactions can lead to greater self-awareness and a deeper understanding of oneself and the world.

In the context of romantic relationships, friendships play a complementary role. While a romantic partner can be a primary source of support and companionship, having a network of friends provides additional emotional resources and diverse perspectives. Maintaining friendships outside of a romantic relationship ensures a well-rounded social support system and prevents over-reliance on a single person for emotional needs.

For many adults, friendships also serve as a crucial support system during major life events such as divorce, loss, or illness. Friends provide comfort, practical assistance, and a sense of continuity during times of upheaval. These supportive friendships can significantly impact one's ability to cope with and recover from life's challenges.

The longevity of adult friendships is often a testament to their quality. Long-term friendships, those that endure over decades, offer a unique and irreplaceable connection. These friendships have weathered life's ups and downs, creating a rich history of shared experiences and memories. The longevity of such relationships reflects mutual commitment, understanding, and resilience.

Chapter 26: Love and Relationships: Building Connections

Love and relationships are fundamental aspects of human existence, deeply influencing our happiness, personal growth, and overall well-being. Building connections in love and relationships involves a complex interplay of emotions, communication, trust, and mutual respect. These connections can be with romantic partners, friends, family members, or even with oneself. Each type of relationship requires effort, understanding, and a willingness to grow together. This exploration will delve into the multifaceted nature of building connections in love and relationships, examining the various stages, challenges, and key components that contribute to their success and longevity.

The foundation of any relationship begins with the initial connection. This initial connection can be sparked by physical attraction, shared interests, or a deep conversation. In romantic relationships, this phase is often marked by excitement and curiosity, as individuals explore the possibilities of a deeper connection. The early stages involve getting to know each other, understanding each other's values, interests, and life goals. This period of discovery sets the stage for building a strong emotional bond.

Effective communication is the cornerstone of building and maintaining connections in love and relationships. Open, honest, and respectful communication allows individuals to express their thoughts, feelings, and needs clearly. It involves active listening, empathy, and the ability to understand and validate each other's perspectives. In romantic relationships, communication helps partners navigate conflicts, make joint decisions, and deepen their emotional intimacy. Similarly, in friendships and family relationships, communication fosters trust, reduces misunderstandings, and strengthens bonds.

Trust is a critical component of any relationship. It is built over time through consistent actions, reliability, and honesty. Trust allows individuals to feel safe and secure, knowing that they can rely on each other in times of need. In romantic relationships, trust is essential for emotional intimacy and vulnerability. It enables partners to share their deepest fears, dreams, and insecurities without fear of judgment or betrayal. Trust also plays a vital role in friendships and family relationships, providing a foundation for mutual support and understanding.

Mutual respect is another essential element in building connections in love and relationships. Respecting each other's individuality, boundaries, and differences fosters a healthy and supportive environment. It involves recognizing and valuing each other's opinions, feelings, and needs. In romantic relationships, mutual respect ensures that both partners feel valued and appreciated. It prevents power imbalances and promotes equality within the relationship. In friendships and family relationships, respect helps maintain harmony and strengthens the bond between individuals.

Emotional intimacy is a profound aspect of building connections in love and relationships. It involves sharing one's inner world, including thoughts, feelings, and experiences, with another person. Emotional intimacy creates a deep sense of closeness and connection. In romantic relationships, it enhances the bond between partners, making them feel understood and cherished. Emotional intimacy also plays a crucial role in friendships and family relationships, fostering a sense of belonging and acceptance.

Building connections in love and relationships also requires effort and intentionality. Relationships do not thrive on autopilot; they require consistent nurturing and care. This involves spending quality time together, engaging in meaningful conversations, and creating shared experiences. In romantic relationships, making time for date nights, vacations, and activities that both partners enjoy strengthens the bond. Similarly, in friendships and family relationships, regular interactions, celebrations, and shared hobbies contribute to maintaining a strong connection.

Conflict resolution is an inevitable part of building connections in love and relationships. Disagreements and misunderstandings are natural, but how they are handled determines the health and longevity of the relationship. Effective conflict resolution involves addressing issues calmly, listening to each other's perspectives, and finding mutually acceptable solutions. It requires patience, empathy, and a willingness to compromise. In romantic relationships, resolving conflicts constructively strengthens the partnership and fosters emotional intimacy. In friendships and family relationships, it prevents resentment and promotes harmony.

Empathy is a vital skill in building connections in love and relationships. It involves understanding and sharing the feelings of another person. Empathy allows individuals to connect on a deeper emotional level, fostering compassion and support. In romantic relationships, empathy helps partners navigate emotional challenges, providing comfort and reassurance. In friendships and family relationships, empathy strengthens bonds by showing that one cares about and understands the other's experiences and emotions.

Shared values and goals are significant factors in building and maintaining connections in love and relationships. When individuals share common values and life goals, it creates a sense of alignment and purpose. In romantic relationships, shared values and goals contribute to long-term compatibility and satisfaction. It ensures that both partners are moving in the same direction and supports their individual and collective growth. In friendships and family relationships, shared values create a strong foundation for mutual respect and understanding.

Maintaining individuality within a relationship is crucial for building healthy connections. While connections are about coming together, it is essential to preserve one's identity and personal interests. Maintaining individuality prevents codependency and promotes personal growth. In romantic relationships, encouraging each other to pursue individual hobbies, careers, and friendships enriches the partnership. It allows each person to bring new experiences and perspectives into the relationship. In friendships and family relationships, respecting each other's individuality fosters mutual appreciation and reduces conflicts.

Physical intimacy is an important aspect of romantic relationships. It involves physical closeness, affection, and sexual connection. Physical intimacy enhances emotional bonds and provides a sense of closeness and comfort. It is a way of expressing love and desire, contributing to the overall satisfaction of the relationship. Maintaining physical intimacy requires open communication about needs and boundaries, ensuring that both partners feel comfortable and fulfilled.

Building connections in love and relationships also involves creating and maintaining traditions and rituals. Traditions and rituals provide a sense of continuity and stability, reinforcing the bond between individuals. In romantic relationships, traditions like anniversary celebrations, holiday rituals, and daily routines create shared memories and a sense of belonging. In friendships and family relationships, traditions such as regular gatherings, annual trips, and cultural practices strengthen the connection and create lasting memories.

Growth and change are inherent in any relationship. As individuals grow and evolve, relationships must adapt to these changes. Embracing growth and change involves being flexible and open to new experiences and perspectives. In romantic relationships, supporting each other's personal growth and adapting to life changes strengthens the bond. It ensures that the relationship remains dynamic and fulfilling. In friendships and family relationships, embracing growth and change allows individuals to continue to connect on meaningful levels, even as their lives evolve.

Forgiveness is a critical aspect of building connections in love and relationships. Mistakes and misunderstandings are inevitable, but holding onto grudges and resentment can damage the relationship. Forgiveness involves letting go of past hurts and moving forward with a positive mindset. It requires empathy, understanding, and a willingness to rebuild trust. In romantic relationships, forgiveness allows partners to heal and strengthen their bond. In friendships and family relationships, it fosters reconciliation and maintains harmony.

Support during difficult times is a hallmark of strong relationships. Life's challenges, such as illness, loss, or personal struggles, test the strength of connections. Providing emotional, practical, and sometimes financial support during these times is crucial. In romantic relationships, standing by each other through hardships deepens emotional intimacy and trust. In friendships and family relationships, offering support reinforces the bond and demonstrates love and care.

Celebrating successes and milestones together enhances the connection in love and relationships. Acknowledging and celebrating each other's achievements, whether big or small, creates a sense of shared joy and pride. In romantic relationships, celebrating milestones such as anniversaries, promotions, or personal achievements strengthens the bond and creates lasting memories. In friendships and family relationships, celebrating successes fosters a sense of community and mutual support.

Finally, building connections in love and relationships involves a commitment to the relationship's long-term success. This commitment requires dedication, effort, and a willingness to work through challenges. It involves prioritizing the relationship, investing time and energy, and continuously seeking ways to improve and strengthen the bond. In romantic relationships, commitment creates a sense of security and trust, ensuring that both partners are invested in the relationship's future. In friendships and family relationships, commitment reinforces the bond and ensures that the relationship remains a priority.

115

Chapter 27: Financial Independence: Money Matters

Financial independence is a crucial milestone in an individual's life, representing more than just the ability to support oneself financially; it encompasses a sense of freedom, security, and the ability to make life choices without being constrained by monetary limitations. The journey to achieving financial independence is multifaceted, involving not only earning and saving but also understanding and managing money effectively. From childhood to adulthood, one's relationship with money evolves significantly, shaped by various experiences, lessons, and influences from family, society, and personal encounters.

During childhood, the foundation of financial understanding is laid, often influenced heavily by parents and guardians. The values and attitudes towards money that parents exhibit can leave a lasting impression. For instance, children who observe their parents budgeting, saving, and making prudent financial decisions are likely to adopt similar habits. Conversely, if financial stress or poor money management is prevalent in the household, children might develop anxiety around money or a lack of financial discipline. This early exposure forms the bedrock of financial literacy, which is crucial for later life stages.

As children grow into teenagers, they start to engage with money more directly, perhaps through allowances, part-time jobs, or chores. This phase is crucial for developing practical money management skills. Teenagers learn the value of money, budgeting, and the importance of saving for desired items or experiences. It's also a time when financial missteps can be valuable learning opportunities. For instance, spending all their earnings impulsively can teach the importance of saving and delayed gratification. During these years, parental guidance remains vital, as does formal education on financial topics, which can equip young people with the knowledge needed to make informed financial decisions.

Entering adulthood, financial independence becomes a primary goal. This stage often coincides with significant life events such as pursuing higher education, starting a career, or moving out of the family home. Each of these milestones presents unique financial challenges and learning opportunities. Higher education, for example, often involves navigating student loans and budgeting for living expenses, which can be a crash course in financial management. Starting a career brings a steady income, but also the responsibility of managing expenses, saving for the future, and possibly starting to pay off any debts accumulated during student years.

The early years of adulthood are critical for establishing a strong financial foundation. Creating and sticking to a budget, building an emergency fund, and beginning to save for long-term goals such as buying a home or retirement are essential steps. These practices not only ensure financial stability but also instill a sense of control and confidence over one's financial future. It's a period where financial habits are solidified, and the importance of financial planning becomes apparent.

Achieving financial independence is also closely tied to understanding credit and debt. Responsible use of credit can be a valuable tool for building a positive credit history, which is crucial for major financial milestones like buying a home. However, mismanaging credit can lead to significant debt, which can hinder financial independence. Learning to balance the use of credit, paying off debts, and avoiding high-interest loans are critical skills. Financial literacy programs and resources can play a significant role in helping young adults navigate these aspects of financial management.

As individuals move further into adulthood, financial independence often includes planning for a family, investing, and saving for retirement. Financial planning becomes more complex, involving strategies for managing income, expenses, investments, and taxes. Setting financial goals, such as saving for children's education, buying property, or planning for retirement, requires a deep understanding of personal finances and investment options. Professional financial advice can be invaluable at this stage, helping to create a comprehensive financial plan that aligns with long-term goals.

Investing is a significant component of achieving and maintaining financial independence. Understanding different investment options, such as stocks, bonds, mutual funds, and real estate, allows individuals to grow their wealth over time. Diversifying investments to manage risk and optimize returns is a key strategy. Additionally, understanding market trends, economic indicators, and the impact of global events on investments can enhance financial decision-making.

Financial independence is not just about accumulating wealth but also about protecting it. This involves having adequate insurance coverage, such as health, life, and property insurance, to safeguard against unforeseen events that could otherwise deplete savings and assets. Estate planning, including wills and trusts, ensures that assets are managed and distributed according to one's wishes, providing peace of mind and financial security for loved ones.

In the pursuit of financial independence, it's important to recognize that it's not solely about the destination but also about the journey. The process involves continuous learning, adapting to changing circumstances, and making informed decisions. Financial independence brings a sense of empowerment, allowing individuals to pursue their passions, support their families, and contribute to their communities without financial constraints.

Chapter 28: Facing Failure: Resilience in Adversity

Facing failure is an intrinsic part of the human experience, and developing resilience in adversity is a vital skill for personal growth and success. From childhood through maturity, individuals encounter various setbacks that shape their character, outlook on life, and capacity to persevere. The ability to confront and navigate failure with resilience is not only crucial for overcoming immediate challenges but also for fostering long-term mental and emotional well-being.

In childhood, the seeds of resilience are sown through early experiences with failure and the support systems in place. Parents, teachers, and caregivers play a significant role in shaping how a child perceives and reacts to failure. A supportive environment where mistakes are seen as learning opportunities rather than just shortcomings can nurture a child's resilience. Encouragement to try again after failing, coupled with positive reinforcement, helps children develop a growth mindset. This mindset is essential for viewing challenges as opportunities for development rather than insurmountable obstacles.

As children grow into adolescents, the academic and social pressures they face can significantly impact their resilience. School is often a primary setting where young people encounter failure, whether through poor grades, athletic defeats, or social rejection. During this period, peer relationships also become more influential, and the ability to bounce back from failures can be tested by the desire for acceptance and belonging. Adolescents benefit from guidance in setting realistic goals, learning effective study habits, and managing time efficiently. Participation in extracurricular activities, where effort and improvement are emphasized over immediate success, can also bolster resilience. Programs that teach coping strategies and emotional regulation can empower teenagers to handle setbacks constructively.

Transitioning to adulthood, the stakes of failure often become higher, with career ambitions, personal relationships, and financial stability coming into play. Young adults face significant decisions and responsibilities, and the ability to remain resilient in the face of failure becomes increasingly important. Whether it's being turned down for a job, experiencing a breakup, or struggling with financial independence, these experiences can be daunting. However, they also provide rich opportunities for growth and self-discovery. Developing resilience at this stage involves cultivating a positive self-concept, building a support network of friends and mentors, and engaging in self-reflection to learn from failures.

One crucial aspect of resilience in adulthood is the ability to reframe failure. Viewing setbacks not as definitive judgments on one's abilities or worth but as valuable feedback can transform the way individuals approach challenges. This reframing involves recognizing that failure is often a precursor to success and that persistence and adaptability are key to overcoming obstacles. Adopting this perspective helps mitigate the fear of failure, encouraging individuals to take risks and pursue their goals despite potential setbacks.

The role of mental health in resilience cannot be overstated. Building resilience involves maintaining mental and emotional well-being through practices such as mindfulness, self-care, and seeking professional support when needed. Mindfulness practices, such as meditation and journaling, can help individuals stay grounded and manage stress. Physical self-care, including regular exercise, a healthy diet, and adequate sleep, supports overall well-being and enhances the capacity to cope with adversity. Additionally, seeking therapy or counseling can provide tools and strategies to manage difficult emotions and build resilience.

Career resilience, specifically, is an essential component of facing failure in adulthood. The modern workplace is characterized by rapid change, and professionals must adapt to new technologies, evolving job roles, and shifting industry landscapes. Career resilience involves continuous learning, skill development, and the ability to pivot when faced with job loss or career setbacks. Networking, mentorship, and professional development opportunities can provide valuable support and guidance during challenging times. Embracing a mindset of lifelong learning and adaptability helps individuals remain resilient and competitive in their careers.

In personal relationships, resilience is vital for maintaining healthy connections and navigating conflicts. Relationships inevitably involve misunderstandings and disagreements, and the ability to work through these challenges is crucial for long-term relational success. Effective communication, empathy, and the willingness to seek resolution rather than avoidance are key components of relational resilience. Building strong, supportive relationships provides a buffer against the stresses of failure in other areas of life, offering emotional support and perspective.

Midlife and beyond present their own unique challenges and opportunities for resilience. Individuals may face significant life transitions such as career changes, the empty nest syndrome, health issues, or the loss of loved ones. At this stage, resilience involves leveraging life experience and wisdom gained from past failures. Older adults often have a deeper understanding of their strengths and limitations, allowing for more strategic and thoughtful responses to adversity. Additionally, engaging in meaningful activities, fostering social connections, and maintaining physical health are crucial for resilience in later life.

Chapter 29: Self-Care: Balancing Mind and Body

Self-care is a multifaceted concept that encompasses practices and routines aimed at maintaining and improving one's mental, emotional, and physical well-being. Balancing mind and body through self-care is essential for overall health and happiness, as it fosters resilience, reduces stress, and enhances quality of life. This balance is achieved by integrating various self-care practices into daily life, addressing the needs of both the mind and body, and recognizing the interdependence of mental and physical health.

From early childhood, self-care practices are often introduced and modeled by caregivers. These early experiences shape one's understanding and approach to self-care throughout life. For children, self-care includes basic routines such as regular sleep, nutritious meals, and physical activity. Encouraging play, creativity, and social interaction are also critical components of self-care for young minds. These activities not only promote physical health but also support cognitive and emotional development. As children grow, teaching them to recognize and express their emotions, manage stress, and engage in relaxing activities can lay a foundation for effective self-care practices in later life.

Adolescence brings new challenges and opportunities for self-care, as teenagers navigate the complexities of growing independence, academic pressures, and social dynamics. During this stage, promoting self-care involves encouraging healthy lifestyle choices, such as regular exercise, balanced nutrition, and adequate sleep. Physical self-care in adolescence is crucial, as it supports growth and development and helps manage stress. Additionally, fostering positive self-esteem and body image, providing resources for mental health support, and encouraging hobbies and interests can significantly contribute to an adolescent's well-being. Educating teenagers about the importance of self-care and providing them with strategies to cope with stress and emotions equips them with tools they will use throughout their lives.

As individuals transition to adulthood, the demands on their time and energy often increase, making self-care more challenging but equally, if not more, important. Balancing work, relationships, and personal responsibilities requires deliberate self-care strategies to maintain mental and physical health. Regular physical activity remains a cornerstone of self-care, as it boosts mood, reduces anxiety, and improves overall health. Adults benefit from finding forms of exercise they enjoy, whether it's going to the gym, hiking, yoga, or dance. Consistent exercise routines help manage stress and keep the body strong and flexible.

Nutrition is another critical aspect of self-care for adults. Eating a balanced diet rich in fruits, vegetables, whole grains, and lean proteins provides the body with the necessary nutrients to function optimally. Mindful eating practices, such as paying attention to hunger and fullness cues and choosing foods that nourish rather than simply satisfy cravings, can prevent overeating and promote a healthy relationship with food. Staying hydrated, limiting processed foods, and moderating caffeine and alcohol intake are also important for maintaining physical health and energy levels.

Mental and emotional self-care for adults involves managing stress, fostering positive relationships, and engaging in activities that bring joy and fulfillment. Mindfulness practices, such as meditation, deep breathing exercises, and yoga, can help reduce stress and increase awareness of the present moment. Regularly setting aside time for relaxation and hobbies, whether it's reading, gardening, painting, or playing a musical instrument, is essential for mental health. Building and maintaining strong social connections provides emotional support, reduces feelings of isolation, and enhances overall well-being. Spending quality time with friends and family, participating in community activities, and seeking out new social opportunities can all contribute to a robust support network.

Professional self-care is another important aspect of balancing mind and body, especially given the significant amount of time adults spend at work. Maintaining a healthy work-life balance, setting boundaries, and taking regular breaks can prevent burnout and enhance productivity. It's important to recognize the signs of stress and burnout, such as fatigue, irritability, and decreased performance, and take proactive steps to address them. Seeking support from colleagues, supervisors, or mental health professionals can be invaluable in managing work-related stress.

For many, spiritual self-care is also a crucial component of overall well-being. This doesn't necessarily mean religious practices but can include any activities that nurture the spirit and provide a sense of purpose and connection. This might involve meditation, spending time in nature, engaging in acts of kindness, or participating in community service. Spiritual self-care helps individuals connect with their values, find meaning in life, and experience a sense of inner peace.

In later adulthood and into the senior years, self-care remains essential but may require adjustments to accommodate changing physical and mental needs. Maintaining physical activity is crucial for mobility, strength, and overall health, but activities may need to be modified to suit individual capabilities. Gentle exercises like walking, swimming, and tai chi can be excellent choices for older adults. Nutrition continues to play a vital role, with an emphasis on nutrient-dense foods that support health and prevent chronic conditions.

Mental and emotional self-care for older adults often involves staying mentally active and socially engaged. Activities such as puzzles, reading, learning new skills, and participating in social clubs or volunteer work can keep the mind sharp and provide a sense of purpose. Emotional well-being is supported by maintaining connections with family and friends, participating in community activities, and seeking support for any mental health issues that may arise. For many seniors, addressing loneliness and isolation is a critical aspect of self-care, as social interactions significantly impact mental health.

In addition to individual practices, creating an environment that supports self-care is important. This includes having a safe and comfortable living space, access to healthcare services, and a supportive community. Policies and programs that promote work-life balance, mental health awareness, and access to recreational facilities can also play a significant role in facilitating self-care for individuals at all stages of life.

Chapter 30: Travel and Exploration: Broadening Horizons

Travel and exploration are fundamental human activities that have the power to profoundly broaden horizons, both literally and figuratively. From childhood curiosity about the world beyond one's immediate surroundings to mature pursuits of cultural enrichment and personal growth, the experiences gained through travel and exploration contribute significantly to shaping one's worldview, expanding knowledge, and fostering empathy. The allure of discovering new places, cultures, and ways of life is a timeless aspect of the human experience, driving individuals to venture beyond their familiar environments in search of adventure, learning, and transformation.

In childhood, the spirit of exploration often begins with simple curiosity about the world. Children are naturally inquisitive, eager to understand their surroundings and the broader world. Family trips, whether to nearby parks, museums, or distant destinations, serve as early introductions to the joys of travel. These experiences can spark a lifelong passion for exploration. Traveling with family provides children with new experiences, exposing them to different landscapes, cultures, and people. These formative experiences can foster a sense of wonder and a desire to learn more about the world, laying the groundwork for a broader perspective as they grow.

As individuals enter adolescence, the scope of travel and exploration often expands. School trips, exchange programs, and family vacations to more diverse destinations offer deeper insights into different ways of life. Adolescents begin to understand the cultural, historical, and social contexts of the places they visit. This period is also a time when young people start to travel more independently, perhaps through programs like summer camps or study abroad opportunities. These experiences promote independence, self-confidence, and adaptability. By navigating new environments, meeting people from diverse backgrounds, and overcoming the challenges of travel, adolescents develop critical life skills and broaden their understanding of the world.

In young adulthood, travel often takes on a more intentional and meaningful dimension. College years, in particular, are a time when many individuals have the opportunity to travel extensively, whether through study abroad programs, backpacking trips, or internships in foreign countries. These experiences can be transformative, providing immersive exposure to different cultures, languages, and worldviews. Studying abroad, for example, allows students to live in another country, gaining firsthand experience of its educational system, lifestyle, and customs. This not only enhances academic learning but also fosters cultural competence and global awareness. Traveling during this stage of life encourages young adults to step out of their comfort zones, embrace new experiences, and develop a more nuanced understanding of the world.

For many, travel in early adulthood is also driven by a desire for adventure and self-discovery. Exploring unfamiliar places, engaging in outdoor activities like hiking, diving, or climbing, and experiencing the thrill of new environments can be exhilarating. These adventures often lead to personal growth, as individuals confront and overcome challenges, build resilience, and gain confidence. The friendships and connections made during these travels can be deep and lasting, as shared experiences in new and often intense environments forge strong bonds.

As individuals progress into their careers, travel often continues to play a significant role, both personally and professionally. Business travel introduces people to different markets, cultures, and business practices, enhancing their professional development and global business acumen. For many professionals, international assignments or collaborations provide valuable opportunities to work in diverse environments, understand global perspectives, and build a network of international contacts. These experiences can enhance career prospects, as the ability to navigate and succeed in different cultural contexts is highly valued in today's interconnected world.

Personal travel during this stage of life often involves balancing the demands of work and family. Many people prioritize travel as a way to unwind, reconnect with loved ones, and create lasting memories. Family vacations become opportunities to bond, educate children about the world, and instill a love of travel and exploration. For those with a passion for travel, integrating it into their lifestyle becomes a way to maintain a sense of adventure and discovery amidst the responsibilities of adult life.

In midlife, travel can take on new meanings and purposes. Many individuals find themselves with more financial stability and the freedom to travel more extensively. This period is often marked by a desire to explore destinations that have long been on their travel bucket lists. Cultural and heritage travel becomes particularly appealing, as people seek to connect with their roots, learn about history, and understand the cultural heritage of different regions. This type of travel provides deeper insights into the forces that shape societies and offers a richer appreciation of global diversity.

Travel in midlife is also often linked to personal growth and enrichment. People may pursue interests and hobbies through travel, such as culinary tours, art and music festivals, or wildlife safaris. These experiences provide a deeper understanding of the world's cultural and natural treasures and offer a sense of fulfillment and joy. Additionally, volunteer travel, where individuals participate in service projects or community development efforts, allows for meaningful engagement with local communities and contributes to a sense of purpose and global citizenship.

As individuals enter later adulthood and retirement, travel can take on an even more leisurely and reflective pace. Many retirees take advantage of their newfound freedom to embark on extended trips, often exploring multiple

destinations in depth. This stage of life allows for a more immersive and unhurried approach to travel, where retirees can spend significant time in different locales, truly absorbing the local culture, history, and lifestyle. The freedom from work schedules and family responsibilities often enables longer stays, whether through extended tours, seasonal relocations, or even living abroad for part of the year.

Travel in retirement is not just about leisure; it also offers numerous health and cognitive benefits. Staying active through travel can improve physical health, while the mental stimulation from navigating new environments, learning new languages, and engaging with different cultures can help maintain cognitive function. The social interactions that come with travel, such as meeting fellow travelers or engaging with local communities, can reduce feelings of isolation and promote emotional well-being.

For many older adults, travel also becomes a way to leave a legacy and share experiences with younger generations. Grandparents may take their grandchildren on trips to teach them about different cultures, histories, and geographies, thereby passing on their love of exploration. These shared experiences can strengthen family bonds and create cherished memories across generations.

Travel and exploration offer countless opportunities for personal growth at any age. They challenge individuals to step outside their comfort zones, adapt to new situations, and overcome obstacles. Each journey, whether it's to a distant land or a nearby town, contributes to a broader perspective on life and a deeper understanding of the world. Through travel, people learn about the diversity and commonalities of human experience, fostering empathy, tolerance, and a sense of global citizenship.

Cultural immersion is a significant aspect of travel that broadens horizons. Engaging with different cultures through food, music, art, and traditions provides a richer understanding of humanity. Trying local cuisines, attending festivals, visiting museums, and interacting with local residents offer insights into the daily lives and values of people from different backgrounds. These experiences can challenge preconceived notions and stereotypes, promoting a more inclusive and empathetic worldview.

Historical exploration also plays a critical role in broadening horizons. Visiting historical sites, monuments, and museums helps individuals understand the events and forces that have shaped societies. Learning about history through travel provides a tangible connection to the past, making historical knowledge more vivid and impactful. It allows travelers to appreciate the complexities of historical narratives and the diverse experiences of people throughout time.

Nature and adventure travel offer unique opportunities to broaden horizons through physical challenges and encounters with the natural world. Whether it's trekking through remote mountains, diving in coral reefs, or exploring dense jungles, these experiences foster a deep appreciation for the planet's biodiversity and the importance of conservation. Adventure travel pushes individuals to test their limits, build resilience, and develop a profound connection with nature.

Solo travel, in particular, can be a powerful means of personal growth and self-discovery. Traveling alone requires individuals to rely on their resourcefulness, make independent decisions, and navigate challenges on their own. This fosters a sense of self-reliance and confidence. Solo travelers often find that they are more open to meeting new people and engaging with their surroundings in ways they might not when traveling with others. The introspection and solitude that come with solo travel can lead to significant personal insights and growth.

Group travel, on the other hand, offers the opportunity to share experiences and learn from others. Traveling with friends, family, or organized groups can enhance social bonds and create shared memories. Group travel often involves collective decision-making and cooperation, which can strengthen relationships and build teamwork skills. It also provides a sense of safety and support, which can be particularly valuable in unfamiliar or challenging environments.

Technology has also transformed the way people travel and explore, making the world more accessible than ever before. The internet, social media, and mobile apps provide a wealth of information about destinations, accommodations, and experiences. Virtual tours and online travel communities allow people to explore new places and connect with fellow travelers from the comfort of their homes. While technology can enhance travel planning and experiences, it is also important to balance its use with mindful and present engagement with the physical world.

Sustainable and responsible travel practices are increasingly important as more people explore the globe. Travelers have a responsibility to respect local cultures, protect natural environments, and contribute positively to the communities they visit. This can involve choosing eco-friendly accommodations, supporting local businesses, minimizing waste, and being mindful of cultural sensitivities. Sustainable travel not only helps preserve destinations for future generations but also enriches the travel experience by fostering deeper connections with places and people.

Chapter 31: Coping with Loss: Grief and Healing

Coping with loss is one of the most profound and challenging experiences in the human journey. Grief, the emotional response to loss, can encompass a wide range of feelings, including sadness, anger, guilt, and despair. Healing from loss involves navigating these emotions and finding ways to adapt to a world that has been irrevocably changed. The process of grieving is highly individual, influenced by personal, cultural, and situational factors, but it universally demands time, support, and self-compassion.

Loss can take many forms: the death of a loved one, the end of a significant relationship, the loss of a job or financial stability, or even the loss of health or a cherished dream. Each type of loss brings its own unique challenges and emotional responses. The death of a loved one is perhaps the most profound and universally recognized form of loss, and it often brings the most intense grief. However, all losses require acknowledgment and grieving, as each represents a significant change and the need to adjust to a new reality.

From childhood, individuals begin to experience loss and learn to cope with it in various ways. A child's first encounter with loss might be the death of a pet, a family move, or a friend moving away. How caregivers support and guide children through these early experiences of loss can profoundly affect their ability to cope with grief later in life. Providing a safe space for children to express their feelings, validating their emotions, and offering comforting rituals can help them process their grief and begin to understand the concept of loss.

As people move into adolescence, the experience of loss can become more complex. The death of a family member or friend during this developmental stage can be particularly challenging, as adolescents are already navigating significant emotional and social changes.

Supportive relationships with family, friends, and mentors are crucial during this time. Adolescents may benefit from talking openly about their feelings, engaging in creative outlets for expression, and participating in activities that provide a sense of continuity and connection.

In adulthood, the nature of loss often shifts to include the death of parents or peers, divorce, job loss, or serious illness. These losses can trigger profound grief and require significant adjustments. The responsibilities of adulthood, such as caregiving roles, financial pressures, and maintaining relationships, can compound the stress of grieving. It is essential for adults to seek support from loved ones, professional counselors, or support groups. Building a network of understanding and compassionate individuals can provide the necessary emotional support and practical assistance during times of grief.

The process of grieving involves several stages, often described in models such as Elisabeth Kübler-Ross's five stages of grief: denial, anger, bargaining, depression, and acceptance. It is important to understand that these stages are not linear and can vary greatly from person to person. Some may experience all these stages, while others might only go through a few, or experience them in a different order. Recognizing that grief is a unique and personal journey helps in accepting one's own process and that of others.

Denial serves as an initial buffer against the shock of loss, allowing individuals time to gradually absorb the reality of their situation. Anger can arise as a natural response to the perceived unfairness of the loss, providing an outlet for the intense emotional energy that grief generates. Bargaining often involves dwelling on "what if" scenarios, reflecting a struggle to regain control in a situation that feels overwhelmingly out of control. Depression represents a deep sense of sadness and mourning for the loss, and it is a natural and necessary part of the grieving process. Acceptance involves coming to terms with the reality of the loss and finding ways to move forward while honoring the memory of what has been lost.

Healing from loss involves both emotional and practical adjustments. Emotionally, it requires allowing oneself to feel the pain of grief, expressing it in healthy ways, and seeking support. This might involve talking about the loss with friends or a therapist, engaging in rituals or memorials, or using creative outlets such as writing, art, or music to process feelings. It is also important to take care of one's physical health, as grief can take a significant toll on the body. Regular exercise, a balanced diet, sufficient sleep, and avoiding harmful coping mechanisms such as substance abuse are crucial.

Practically, adapting to loss often involves making significant changes in one's life. This might include managing the financial and legal aspects of a loved one's death, finding new employment after job loss, or adjusting to daily life with a chronic illness or disability. Developing new routines and finding new sources of meaning and purpose are important steps in rebuilding a sense of stability and control.

Cultural and spiritual beliefs play a significant role in how individuals cope with loss and grief. Different cultures have varied rituals, traditions, and practices for mourning and commemorating the dead. These can provide a framework for expressing grief and finding comfort. Spiritual or religious beliefs can also offer solace, providing a sense of connection to something greater than oneself and a way to make sense of the loss. Participating in community rituals, such as funerals, memorial services, or religious ceremonies, can offer support and a sense of shared experience.

In the workplace, addressing loss and grief is also important, as it affects both the individual and their professional environment. Employers and colleagues can support grieving individuals by acknowledging their loss, offering flexibility with work schedules, and providing resources such as employee assistance programs or counseling services. Creating a compassionate and supportive workplace culture can help individuals navigate their grief while maintaining their professional responsibilities.

Grief does not have a fixed timeline, and the intensity of grief can fluctuate over time. Anniversaries, birthdays, holidays, and other significant dates can trigger renewed waves of grief, even years after the loss. It is important to recognize and honor these moments, allowing oneself to feel and express emotions as they arise. Finding ways to commemorate and celebrate the memory of a loved one or the significance of what has been lost can help keep their presence alive in a meaningful way.

In recent years, there has been growing recognition of the importance of mental health support for those coping with loss. Therapy and counseling can provide a safe space to explore feelings, develop coping strategies, and find a path to healing. Grief counseling, in particular, is designed to help individuals process their loss, understand their grief reactions, and integrate the experience into their lives. Support groups also offer a valuable opportunity to connect with others who have experienced similar losses, providing mutual understanding and support.

In the digital age, online resources and virtual support communities have become increasingly important. Websites, forums, and social media groups dedicated to grief support can provide information, comfort, and a sense of community for those who may feel isolated in their grief. Virtual counseling and therapy services offer accessible support for individuals who may not have access to in-person services.

For those supporting someone who is grieving, it is important to offer presence, patience, and empathy. Listening without judgment, acknowledging their pain, and being available for support can make a significant difference. It is also helpful to avoid offering clichéd or minimizing statements, instead expressing genuine care and understanding. Providing practical support, such as helping with daily tasks or accompanying them to appointments or events, can also be valuable.

Chapter 32: Mental Health: Breaking the Stigma

Mental health is an essential component of overall well-being, encompassing emotional, psychological, and social aspects of life. Despite its importance, mental health has historically been shrouded in stigma, a significant barrier to individuals seeking help and receiving the care they need. Breaking the stigma associated with mental health is crucial for fostering an environment where people feel comfortable discussing their struggles, accessing treatment, and supporting one another.

Stigma surrounding mental health can be understood as negative attitudes, beliefs, and stereotypes that lead to discrimination against individuals with mental health issues. This stigma manifests in several ways, including societal stigma, self-stigma, and institutional stigma. Societal stigma involves widespread prejudices and misconceptions about mental health conditions, often perpetuated by media portrayals and cultural narratives. Self-stigma occurs when individuals internalize these negative beliefs, leading to feelings of shame and worthlessness. Institutional stigma is evident in systemic practices and policies that disadvantage those with mental health conditions, such as inadequate funding for mental health services or discriminatory practices in the workplace.

The roots of mental health stigma can be traced back centuries. Historically, mental illnesses were often misunderstood and attributed to supernatural causes, moral failings, or character flaws. These misconceptions led to the marginalization and mistreatment of individuals with mental health issues. Even as scientific understanding of mental health has advanced, remnants of these outdated beliefs persist, contributing to ongoing stigma.

Breaking the stigma around mental health requires a multifaceted approach that addresses societal attitudes, promotes education, and implements supportive policies. Public awareness campaigns play a crucial role in challenging misconceptions and encouraging open conversations about mental health. These campaigns aim to humanize mental health issues by sharing personal stories, highlighting the prevalence of mental health conditions, and emphasizing that seeking help is a sign of strength, not weakness.

Education is another vital component in reducing stigma. Integrating mental health education into school curriculums can foster early understanding and acceptance, teaching children about mental health in the same way they learn about physical health. Educational programs should also be extended to workplaces, community organizations, and healthcare providers to ensure that everyone is equipped with the knowledge to support mental health.

Media representation significantly influences public perception of mental health. Historically, media portrayals of mental illness have often been negative and sensationalized, reinforcing harmful stereotypes. However, there has been a shift towards more accurate and empathetic representations in recent years. Positive portrayals of characters with mental health issues, as well as stories that depict recovery and resilience, can help normalize mental health struggles and reduce stigma.

Supportive policies and practices within institutions are essential for creating an environment where individuals feel safe to seek help. This includes ensuring access to affordable and comprehensive mental health care, providing mental health training for healthcare professionals, and implementing workplace policies that promote mental well-being. Employers can contribute by offering mental health benefits, creating supportive work environments, and encouraging employees to take mental health days.

Peer support is another powerful tool in breaking the stigma around mental health. Peer support groups and networks provide individuals with a safe space to share their experiences and offer mutual support. These groups can help reduce feelings of isolation and validate individuals' experiences, demonstrating that they are not alone in their struggles. Peer support also fosters a sense of community and empowerment, as individuals learn from others who have faced similar challenges.

Addressing self-stigma is crucial for individuals to feel comfortable seeking help and embracing their mental health journey. Self-stigma often stems from internalizing negative societal beliefs about mental health. Combatting self-stigma involves fostering self-compassion, challenging negative self-talk, and recognizing the value of seeking support. Therapy, support groups, and educational resources can help individuals develop a more positive self-perception and build resilience against self-stigma.

The role of language in shaping attitudes towards mental health cannot be overstated. The words we use to describe mental health conditions and those who experience them significantly impact stigma. Using person-first language, such as "a person with schizophrenia" rather than "a schizophrenic," emphasizes the individuality and humanity of the person rather than defining them by their condition. Avoiding derogatory terms and phrases that trivialize mental health issues, such as "crazy" or "insane," is also important in promoting respectful and supportive communication.

Cultural competence is vital in addressing mental health stigma within diverse communities. Different cultural backgrounds can influence how mental health is perceived and discussed. Some cultures may have specific beliefs and practices related to mental health that need to be understood and respected. Providing culturally sensitive mental health services and involving community leaders in stigma-reduction efforts can enhance the effectiveness of these initiatives.

The role of mental health professionals in breaking stigma is multifaceted. They not only provide direct care to individuals but also serve as advocates and educators within their communities. Mental health professionals can help normalize mental health discussions, educate the public about mental health conditions, and advocate for systemic changes that support mental health. They can also work to reduce stigma within their own field by promoting inclusive and non-judgmental attitudes among colleagues.

Advocacy and activism are powerful means of challenging systemic stigma and promoting mental health equity. Grassroots organizations, advocacy groups, and mental health activists work tirelessly to raise awareness, push for policy changes, and support individuals with mental health conditions. These efforts can lead to significant improvements in mental health care access, funding, and public attitudes.

Personal storytelling is a potent tool for breaking stigma. Sharing personal experiences with mental health struggles can humanize the issue and foster empathy and understanding. These stories can be shared through various platforms, including social media, blogs, public speaking events, and books. Hearing from individuals who have navigated mental health challenges and found pathways to recovery can inspire others and reduce feelings of shame and isolation.

Breaking the stigma around mental health is an ongoing and collective effort. It requires the involvement of individuals, communities, institutions, and governments. By challenging misconceptions, promoting education, and implementing supportive policies, we can create a society where mental health is openly discussed and treated with the same importance as physical health. Everyone has a role to play in this endeavor, from advocating for better mental health policies to offering support and understanding to those around us.

The impact of reducing mental health stigma extends beyond individual well-being. It contributes to healthier, more inclusive communities where everyone can thrive. When people feel safe to seek help and discuss their mental health, it leads to earlier intervention, better treatment outcomes, and a reduction in the overall burden of mental health conditions. It also fosters a culture of empathy and support, where people are more likely to look out for one another and provide the necessary care and understanding.

Chapter 33: Conflict Resolution: Navigating Disagreements

Conflict resolution is a critical skill in navigating disagreements effectively and maintaining healthy relationships, whether they are personal, professional, or communal. Conflict, an inevitable part of human interaction, arises from differing needs, values, perceptions, and interests. The ability to manage and resolve conflicts constructively can lead to personal growth, stronger relationships, and more productive environments. Understanding the nature of conflict, the processes involved in resolution, and the strategies for managing disputes are essential for navigating disagreements successfully.

Conflict often begins with a disagreement or difference of opinion. It can escalate if not addressed appropriately, leading to negative emotions, strained relationships, and even long-term animosity. The sources of conflict are varied and can include competition for resources, power imbalances, differing values or beliefs, poor communication, and personality clashes. Recognizing the underlying causes of conflict is the first step in resolving it effectively.

Effective conflict resolution requires a combination of skills, including active listening, empathy, assertiveness, and problem-solving. Active listening involves fully concentrating on what the other person is saying, understanding their perspective, and responding thoughtfully. It is essential for creating an environment where all parties feel heard and valued. Empathy, the ability to understand and share the feelings of another, helps in acknowledging the emotions involved in the conflict and fosters a sense of connection and mutual respect.

Assertiveness is the ability to express one's own needs, thoughts, and feelings in a clear and respectful manner. It is different from aggression, which involves imposing one's will on others, and from passivity, which involves neglecting one's own needs. Assertiveness allows individuals to advocate for themselves while also respecting the needs and rights of others. Problem-solving involves identifying the root causes of the conflict and working collaboratively to find mutually acceptable solutions.

One of the most effective models for understanding and resolving conflicts is the interest-based relational approach. This model focuses on the underlying interests and needs of the parties involved, rather than their positions or demands. By exploring the interests behind the positions, parties can often find common ground and develop solutions that satisfy everyone's needs. This approach emphasizes collaboration, mutual respect, and a focus on the future rather than past grievances.

Communication plays a central role in conflict resolution. Poor communication often exacerbates conflicts, while effective communication can help resolve them. Clear, open, and respectful communication is essential for expressing needs and concerns, understanding others' perspectives, and negotiating solutions. Nonverbal communication, such as body language and tone of voice, also plays a significant role in conveying messages and emotions. Being aware of nonverbal cues can help in understanding the underlying emotions and intentions of the other party.

Conflict resolution strategies can be broadly categorized into five styles: competing, collaborating, compromising, avoiding, and accommodating. Each style has its own strengths and weaknesses, and the appropriate style depends on the context and the nature of the conflict. Competing involves assertively pursuing one's own interests at the expense of others. It is appropriate in situations where quick, decisive action is needed, such as in emergencies or when enforcing unpopular rules. However, it can lead to resentment and further conflict if used excessively. Collaborating involves working together with the other party to find a solution that satisfies everyone's needs. It is the most constructive approach and leads to long-term resolution and stronger relationships. However, it can be time-consuming and may not be practical in all situations. Compromising involves finding a middle ground where each party gives up something to reach a mutually acceptable solution. It is useful when the goals are moderately important and time is limited. However, it may not fully satisfy either party and can lead to suboptimal solutions. Avoiding involves ignoring the conflict or withdrawing from the situation. It can be appropriate when the conflict is trivial, when more information is needed, or when the situation is emotionally charged and a cooling-off period is necessary. However, it can lead to unresolved issues and festering resentment if used habitually. Accommodating involves giving in to the other party's needs and concerns at the expense of one's own. It is useful when the issue is more important to the other party or when maintaining harmony is more important than winning. However, it can lead to feelings of resentment and power imbalances if used excessively.

Conflict resolution processes can take many forms, including negotiation, mediation, arbitration, and conciliation. Negotiation is a direct dialogue between the parties to reach an agreement. Effective negotiation involves preparation, clear communication, and a focus on interests rather than positions. It requires flexibility and a willingness to compromise. Mediation involves a neutral third party who helps the disputing parties communicate and explore solutions. The mediator facilitates the discussion but does not impose a decision. Mediation is often used in family disputes, workplace conflicts, and community disagreements. Arbitration involves a neutral third party who listens to both sides and makes a binding decision. It is more formal than mediation and is often used in legal and contractual disputes. Arbitration can be faster and less costly than litigation but may not provide the same level of control over the outcome for the parties involved. Conciliation is similar to mediation, but the conciliator plays a more active role in proposing solutions and encouraging the parties to reach an agreement. It is often used in labor disputes and international conflicts.

Developing a conflict resolution plan can help manage disagreements effectively. The plan should include steps such as identifying the problem, understanding the interests of both parties, generating options for solutions, and agreeing on a course of action. It should also involve setting ground rules for communication, such as speaking respectfully, avoiding interruptions, and staying focused on the issue at hand.

Conflict resolution is not just about solving the immediate problem but also about building and maintaining healthy relationships. It involves ongoing efforts to improve communication, foster trust, and create an environment where differences are valued and managed constructively. It requires self-awareness, emotional intelligence, and a commitment to personal growth. In personal relationships, conflict resolution is essential for maintaining intimacy and trust. Unresolved conflicts can lead to resentment, distance, and a breakdown of the relationship. Couples, families, and friends need to develop effective communication skills, practice empathy, and work collaboratively to resolve conflicts. This may involve seeking counseling or therapy to address deep-seated issues and improve relationship dynamics. In the workplace, conflict resolution is critical for creating a productive and harmonious environment. Conflicts between colleagues, managers, and teams can affect morale, productivity, and overall job satisfaction. Organizations should provide training in conflict resolution skills, create policies that promote respectful communication, and offer resources such as employee assistance programs. Leaders play a crucial role in modeling effective conflict resolution behaviors and fostering a culture of collaboration and respect.

In communities, conflict resolution is essential for fostering social cohesion and addressing issues such as discrimination, inequality, and resource allocation. Community mediation programs, restorative justice initiatives, and public forums for dialogue can help address conflicts and build a sense of shared responsibility and understanding. On a global scale, conflict resolution is vital for addressing international disputes and promoting peace. Diplomatic negotiations, peacebuilding efforts, and international organizations play key roles in resolving conflicts between nations. Understanding cultural differences, building trust, and promoting dialogue are essential for successful conflict resolution in the international arena.

Conflict resolution is a multifaceted and dynamic process that involves understanding the nature of conflict, developing effective communication skills, and employing appropriate strategies and processes. It is essential for maintaining healthy relationships, productive workplaces, cohesive communities, and a peaceful world. By recognizing the value of conflict resolution and committing to continuous learning and improvement, individuals and organizations can navigate disagreements constructively and create environments where differences are managed positively and collaboratively.

Chapter 34: Personal Triumphs: Celebrating Success

Personal triumphs are the milestones of success and achievement that punctuate the journey of life, providing a sense of accomplishment, fulfillment, and joy. Celebrating these successes is essential for personal growth, motivation, and mental well-being. The process of setting goals, overcoming challenges, and achieving milestones is deeply intertwined with the development of self-esteem, resilience, and a positive outlook on life. Recognizing and celebrating personal triumphs not only honors the effort and dedication involved but also reinforces the behaviors and attitudes that lead to success.

The concept of success is highly individual and subjective, varying greatly from one person to another. For some, personal triumphs may be defined by career achievements, such as earning a promotion, completing a significant project, or starting a successful business. For others, success might be measured by personal development milestones, such as learning a new skill, overcoming a fear, or achieving a health goal. Academic accomplishments, artistic endeavors, athletic feats, and community contributions are other areas where individuals might experience personal triumphs. Regardless of the specific nature of the achievement, the common thread is the sense of pride and satisfaction that comes from reaching a goal.

Setting and achieving goals is a fundamental aspect of experiencing personal triumphs. The process begins with identifying what one wants to achieve and then creating a plan to reach that objective. Goals provide direction and purpose, helping individuals focus their efforts and resources on what truly matters to them. Effective goal-setting involves establishing clear, specific, and attainable objectives. The SMART criteria—specific, measurable, achievable, relevant, and time-bound—are widely used to ensure that goals are well-defined and attainable. By setting realistic and meaningful goals, individuals can chart a path towards success and measure their progress along the way.

The journey towards achieving personal triumphs is often fraught with challenges and obstacles. Overcoming these difficulties is an integral part of the triumph itself. The ability to persist in the face of adversity, to adapt to changing circumstances, and to maintain a positive attitude are all critical components of resilience. Resilience is the capacity to recover quickly from setbacks and to keep moving forward despite difficulties. It is built through experiences of overcoming challenges and learning from failures. Each time an individual faces a hurdle and surmounts it, their resilience is strengthened, making them better equipped to handle future challenges.

The role of mindset in achieving personal triumphs cannot be overstated. A growth mindset, as opposed to a fixed mindset, is characterized by the belief that abilities and intelligence can be developed through effort, learning, and perseverance. Individuals with a growth mindset view challenges as opportunities for growth and are more likely to embrace learning and persist in the face of setbacks. This attitude fosters a greater likelihood of achieving success and experiencing personal triumphs. Conversely, a fixed mindset, which views abilities as static and unchangeable, can hinder progress and lead to avoidance of challenges and fear of failure.

Celebrating personal triumphs is an important aspect of the success journey. Celebrations provide an opportunity to acknowledge the hard work, dedication, and perseverance that went into achieving a goal. They also offer a moment to reflect on the journey, recognizing the lessons learned and the personal growth that has occurred. Celebrations can take many forms, from private moments of reflection and gratitude to public acknowledgments and festivities with friends and family. Regardless of the form, the act of celebrating reinforces the positive feelings associated with success and motivates individuals to continue striving for their goals.

One of the benefits of celebrating personal triumphs is the positive impact it has on self-esteem. Self-esteem is the overall sense of value and self-worth that an individual holds. Achievements and successes contribute to a positive self-image and a sense of competence and capability. Each personal triumph adds to the reservoir of positive experiences that bolster self-esteem. Conversely, failing to acknowledge and celebrate successes can lead to feelings of inadequacy and undervaluation of one's efforts and abilities.

Another important aspect of celebrating personal triumphs is the reinforcement of positive behaviors and attitudes. The process of achieving a goal often involves hard work, discipline, perseverance, and resilience. By celebrating successes, individuals reinforce these positive traits and behaviors, making

them more likely to employ them in future endeavors. This positive reinforcement cycle encourages continued effort and persistence, fostering a proactive and determined approach to life's challenges.

The social dimension of celebrating personal triumphs is also significant. Sharing successes with others, whether with family, friends, colleagues, or a broader community, enhances the joy of achievement. Social celebrations can strengthen relationships, create a sense of belonging, and provide mutual encouragement. The support and recognition from others can validate the individual's efforts and boost their confidence. Moreover, sharing stories of success can inspire and motivate others, creating a ripple effect of positivity and ambition within a community.

Recognition and celebration of personal triumphs also play a crucial role in mental well-being. Achieving goals and experiencing success triggers the release of dopamine, a neurotransmitter associated with feelings of pleasure and satisfaction. This biological response not only enhances mood but also reinforces the neural pathways associated with goal-directed behavior. Regularly experiencing and celebrating successes can contribute to a more positive and optimistic outlook on life, reducing stress and enhancing overall mental health.

The act of celebration itself can take many forms, tailored to the individual's preferences and the nature of the achievement. For some, a simple act of self-reward, such as indulging in a favorite treat or taking a day off, might be sufficient. For others, more elaborate celebrations involving social gatherings, special events, or even travel might be appropriate. The key is to ensure that the celebration feels meaningful and acknowledges the significance of the achievement. Personalized celebrations that resonate with the individual's values and preferences are more likely to provide a sense of fulfillment and joy.

Reflecting on personal triumphs is another valuable practice. Taking time to contemplate the journey to success, the obstacles overcome, and the lessons learned can deepen the sense of achievement and provide valuable insights for future endeavors. Reflective practices, such as journaling or discussing experiences with a mentor or trusted friend, can help individuals internalize their successes and derive deeper meaning from their accomplishments. Reflection also allows for the recognition of personal growth, highlighting how far one has come and reinforcing the belief in one's capabilities.

It's important to recognize that personal triumphs do not always have to be monumental achievements. Small victories, such as making progress on a difficult task, forming a new positive habit, or improving in a particular skill, also deserve celebration. These small successes contribute to the larger journey of personal development and can provide the motivation needed to tackle bigger challenges. Celebrating small wins helps maintain momentum and keeps individuals motivated and engaged in their goals.

Balancing the celebration of personal triumphs with humility is also important. While it's essential to acknowledge and take pride in one's achievements, it's equally important to remain grounded and aware of the contributions of others who may have supported the journey. Recognizing the role of mentors, peers, family, and friends in one's successes fosters gratitude and strengthens social bonds. It also ensures that the celebration remains a positive and inclusive experience, rather than becoming a source of arrogance or entitlement.

Moreover, personal triumphs often come with valuable lessons that can be shared with others. Whether it's insights gained from overcoming challenges, strategies for effective goal-setting, or experiences of resilience and perseverance, sharing these lessons can provide guidance and inspiration to others. This sharing of knowledge and experience creates a culture of mutual support and collective growth, enhancing the overall well-being of the community.

In professional settings, celebrating personal triumphs can contribute to a positive organizational culture. Recognizing and rewarding employees' achievements fosters a sense of appreciation and motivation, leading to increased job satisfaction and productivity. Public acknowledgments, awards, and incentives can reinforce desired behaviors and contribute to a culture of excellence. Furthermore, celebrating team successes can strengthen collaboration and camaraderie, creating a more cohesive and supportive work environment.

In educational contexts, recognizing and celebrating students' achievements is crucial for fostering a love of learning and a growth mindset. Celebrations can take many forms, from praise and positive feedback to awards and special events. Encouraging students to reflect on their successes and the effort involved helps build self-confidence and resilience. It also reinforces the value of hard work and perseverance, encouraging students to continue striving for excellence.

Personal triumphs are not limited to individual achievements. Collective successes, such as those achieved by teams, groups, or communities, also deserve celebration. Whether it's a successful project completion, a community event, or a collaborative effort, recognizing and celebrating these achievements fosters a sense of unity and shared purpose. It strengthens the bonds between members and creates a sense of collective pride and accomplishment.

In the broader context of life, celebrating personal triumphs contributes to a richer and more fulfilling experience. Life is filled with challenges and uncertainties, and the moments of success and achievement provide the highlights that make the journey worthwhile. By taking the time to acknowledge and celebrate these moments, individuals can enhance their overall sense of well-being and create lasting memories of joy and accomplishment.

Chapter 35: Life's Unpredictability: Embracing Change

Life's unpredictability is an inherent aspect of the human experience, often presenting unexpected challenges and opportunities. Embracing change, therefore, becomes essential for personal growth, resilience, and adaptability. The ability to navigate the uncertainties of life with an open mind and a flexible attitude can lead to profound transformations and enrich one's journey. Understanding the nature of change, developing strategies to cope with it, and recognizing its potential benefits are crucial steps in embracing the unpredictable nature of life.

Change is constant and inevitable. It manifests in various forms, from major life events such as career shifts, relationship changes, and health issues, to everyday occurrences like alterations in routines or unexpected news. The unpredictability of life can be daunting, often triggering feelings of anxiety, fear, and resistance. These emotions are natural responses to uncertainty and the perceived loss of control. However, learning to embrace change rather than resist it can transform these challenges into opportunities for growth and development.

The first step in embracing life's unpredictability is to develop a mindset that is open to change. This involves recognizing that change is a natural part of life and that it can bring both positive and negative experiences. An open mindset allows individuals to view change as an opportunity rather than a threat. It encourages curiosity, exploration, and a willingness to adapt. Cultivating such a mindset can be achieved through practices like mindfulness, meditation, and self-reflection, which help individuals stay present and grounded in the face of uncertainty.

Resilience is a key factor in coping with life's unpredictability. Resilience is the ability to bounce back from adversity and adapt to change. It is built through experiences of overcoming difficulties and learning from them. Resilient individuals possess qualities such as optimism, perseverance, and a strong sense of self-efficacy. They are able to maintain a positive outlook, even in challenging situations, and are more likely to view setbacks as temporary and manageable. Developing resilience involves building a support network, practicing self-care, and fostering a sense of purpose and meaning in life.

Flexibility is another important aspect of embracing change. Flexibility involves being able to adjust one's plans, expectations, and behaviors in response to new circumstances. It requires a willingness to let go of rigid thinking and embrace new perspectives. Flexible individuals are more likely to find creative solutions to problems and are better equipped to handle the uncertainties of life. Developing flexibility involves practicing adaptability, seeking out new experiences, and being open to feedback and learning.

One effective strategy for embracing life's unpredictability is to focus on what can be controlled and to let go of what cannot. This involves identifying the aspects of a situation that are within one's control, such as one's attitudes, behaviors, and responses, and accepting those that are beyond control, such as external events or other people's actions. Focusing on what can be controlled allows individuals to take proactive steps towards positive change and to feel empowered in the face of uncertainty. It also helps to reduce feelings of helplessness and frustration.

Another important strategy is to develop a strong sense of purpose and direction. Having a clear sense of one's values, goals, and priorities provides a stable foundation in the midst of change. It allows individuals to stay focused on what truly matters to them and to make decisions that are aligned with their long-term vision. A strong sense of purpose can also provide motivation and resilience during challenging times. Developing this sense of purpose involves regular reflection on one's values and goals, setting meaningful objectives, and pursuing activities that are aligned with one's passions and interests.

Embracing life's unpredictability also involves learning to manage stress and anxiety. Change and uncertainty can be significant sources of stress, but developing effective coping mechanisms can help individuals manage these feelings. Techniques such as deep breathing, progressive muscle relaxation, and visualization can help to reduce physical and emotional tension. Regular physical activity, a healthy diet, and adequate sleep are also important for maintaining overall well-being and resilience. Additionally, seeking support from friends, family, or a mental health professional can provide valuable assistance in managing stress and navigating change.

Another important aspect of embracing change is to view it as an opportunity for growth and learning. Change often brings new experiences, challenges, and opportunities that can lead to personal development. By approaching change with a learning mindset, individuals can gain new skills, knowledge, and perspectives. This can enhance their adaptability and resilience, making them better equipped to handle future changes. Embracing a learning mindset involves being curious, open to new experiences, and willing to take risks and make mistakes.

Building strong relationships and a supportive network is also crucial for navigating life's unpredictability. Having a network of supportive friends, family, and colleagues provides emotional support, practical assistance, and a sense of belonging. These relationships can provide a buffer against the stresses of change and can offer valuable resources and insights. Building and maintaining strong relationships involves regular communication, showing appreciation and gratitude, and being there for others in times of need.

Embracing change also involves letting go of the past and being willing to move forward. This can be challenging, especially when the past involves significant losses or disappointments. However, holding onto the past can prevent individuals from fully engaging with the present and embracing new opportunities. Letting go involves accepting what has happened, forgiving oneself and others, and focusing on the present and future. It can be helpful to engage in practices such as journaling, therapy, or rituals that provide closure and allow for emotional release.

Another important aspect of embracing life's unpredictability is to maintain a sense of humor and perspective. Humor can be a powerful coping mechanism, helping to reduce stress and provide a different perspective on challenging situations. It allows individuals to take themselves less seriously and to find joy and laughter even in difficult times. Maintaining perspective involves recognizing that change is a normal part of life and that setbacks and challenges are opportunities for growth. It involves focusing on the bigger picture and not getting overwhelmed by temporary difficulties.

Lastly, embracing change involves taking action and being proactive. Rather than waiting for change to happen, individuals can take steps to create the changes they want to see in their lives. This involves setting goals, making plans, and taking concrete actions towards those goals. Being proactive allows individuals to feel more in control of their lives and to create positive change. It also involves being willing to take risks and to step out of one's comfort zone.

Chapter 36: Parenthood: Raising the Next Generation

Parenthood is one of the most profound and significant roles a person can undertake, entailing the responsibility of raising the next generation. It is a journey marked by immense joy, profound challenges, and deep learning experiences. The process of nurturing and guiding a child from infancy to adulthood involves a complex interplay of physical care, emotional support, moral guidance, and education. Each stage of a child's development presents unique demands and rewards, requiring parents to adapt and grow alongside their children.

From the moment a child is born, the journey of parenthood begins with the basics of providing for the infant's needs. This includes feeding, diapering, and ensuring the baby's comfort and safety. During the early months, a strong bond is formed through close physical contact, eye contact, and responsive caregiving. This period is crucial for the development of attachment, which lays the foundation for the child's emotional security and trust in the world. Parents must be attuned to their baby's cues and needs, responding with warmth and consistency to foster a sense of safety and belonging.

As children grow into toddlers, their increasing mobility and curiosity present new challenges and opportunities for parents. This stage is characterized by rapid development in motor skills, language, and social interaction. Parents must balance the need to keep their children safe with the importance of allowing them to explore and learn from their environment. Setting boundaries, while encouraging independence, helps toddlers develop a sense of autonomy and confidence. This is also a time when children begin to assert their will, and parents must navigate the complexities of discipline, teaching their children about acceptable behavior and self-control.

The preschool years bring further cognitive and social development. Children become more aware of their emotions and the emotions of others. They start forming friendships and learning to cooperate and share. Parents play a crucial role in modeling positive social interactions and teaching empathy and emotional regulation. Engaging in play, reading together, and encouraging imaginative activities support cognitive growth and language skills. Providing a structured environment with predictable routines helps children feel secure and understand what is expected of them.

When children enter school, the focus of parenthood expands to include supporting their academic and social success. Parents must collaborate with teachers and school staff to ensure their children receive a quality education and address any learning or behavioral challenges that may arise. Encouraging a love of learning, fostering curiosity, and helping children develop good study habits are essential during this stage. Parents also need to support their children in navigating social dynamics, including forming friendships, dealing with peer pressure, and managing conflicts.

Adolescence brings significant physical, emotional, and cognitive changes. Teenagers strive for independence and identity, often challenging parental authority and testing boundaries. This can be a turbulent time for both parents and adolescents, as they renegotiate their relationship. Effective communication becomes paramount, with parents needing to listen actively, provide guidance, and set appropriate limits while respecting their teenager's growing autonomy. Supporting adolescents in making responsible choices about health, relationships, and future goals is crucial. Encouraging open dialogue about topics such as substance use, sexuality, and mental health helps teenagers make informed decisions and fosters trust.

Throughout all stages of development, parents must be mindful of their role in shaping their children's values and character. Teaching kindness, respect, responsibility, and integrity is a continuous process that involves both direct instruction and modeling these values through everyday actions. Parents must also instill a sense of cultural identity and belonging, helping their children understand and appreciate their heritage and the diversity of the world around them.

Parenthood also involves providing emotional support and stability. Children need to know they are loved unconditionally and that their parents are there for them, no matter what challenges they face. This emotional foundation is critical for building self-esteem, resilience, and a positive self-concept. Parents must be attuned to their children's emotional needs, offering comfort, encouragement, and understanding during times of stress or difficulty.

One of the significant challenges of parenthood is balancing the demands of raising children with other responsibilities, such as work, household duties, and personal needs. Time management, delegation, and self-care are essential skills for parents to develop. It is important for parents to take care of their own physical and mental health, as their well-being directly affects their ability to care for their children. Seeking support from partners, family members, and community resources can help alleviate some of the pressures of parenthood.

Financial stability is another important aspect of raising children. Providing for a child's needs requires careful planning and budgeting. This includes not only basic necessities such as food, clothing, and shelter but also education, extracurricular activities, and future financial security. Parents must make decisions about saving for college, managing household expenses, and planning for emergencies. Financial literacy and planning are crucial skills that parents must also pass on to their children, teaching them the value of money, saving, and responsible spending.

In today's digital age, parents face the additional challenge of managing their children's exposure to technology and media. While technology offers many educational and recreational benefits, it also poses risks such as excessive screen time, cyberbullying, and exposure to inappropriate content. Parents must set guidelines for technology use, monitor their children's online activities, and educate them about digital citizenship and internet safety. Finding a balance between embracing the positive aspects of technology and protecting children from its potential harms is an ongoing task.

Parenthood is not a one-size-fits-all experience; it is influenced by various factors such as cultural background, socioeconomic status, and personal beliefs. Different parenting styles, such as authoritative, authoritarian, permissive, and uninvolved, reflect diverse approaches to raising children. Each style has its own set of practices and philosophies about discipline, communication, and nurturing. Understanding the strengths and limitations of different parenting styles can help parents choose the approach that best meets their children's needs and promotes healthy development.

Support systems play a crucial role in parenthood. Extended family, friends, community organizations, and professional services provide valuable resources and assistance. Parenting groups, workshops, and counseling services can offer guidance, education, and emotional support. Building a strong support network helps parents navigate the challenges of raising children and provides a sense of community and shared experience.

As children grow into adulthood, the role of parents evolves. While the need for direct care and supervision diminishes, parents continue to provide support and guidance as their children navigate higher education, career choices, relationships, and other adult responsibilities. The parent-child relationship becomes more of a partnership, with mutual respect and understanding. Parents must learn to let go, allowing their children to make their own decisions and learn from their experiences, while still being available for advice and support.

Ultimately, parenthood is a journey of continuous learning and adaptation. No parent is perfect, and mistakes are inevitable. The key is to approach parenthood with humility, openness, and a willingness to grow. Reflecting on one's parenting practices, seeking feedback, and making adjustments as needed are important aspects of effective parenting. Celebrating successes, no matter how small, and finding joy in the everyday moments of parenting contribute to a positive and fulfilling experience.

Parenthood is also a journey of immense love and joy. The bond between parent and child is one of the deepest and most enduring relationships in life. The joys of parenthood include witnessing a child's first steps, hearing their first words, celebrating their achievements, and sharing in their dreams and aspirations. The love and connection between parent and child are sources of profound happiness and fulfillment.

Chapter 37: Career Growth: Ambition and Satisfaction

Career growth is a multifaceted journey that encompasses the pursuit of professional advancement, the fulfillment of personal ambitions, and the achievement of satisfaction and fulfillment in one's work life. It is influenced by a variety of factors including individual aspirations, opportunities for development, organizational support, and the broader economic and social context. Understanding the dynamics of career growth involves exploring the interplay between ambition and satisfaction, and how these elements contribute to a fulfilling and successful career trajectory.

Ambition is a driving force behind career growth. It represents an individual's desire to achieve certain goals, attain higher positions, and reach their full potential in their professional life. Ambitious individuals are often characterized by their proactive attitude, willingness to take risks, and commitment to continuous improvement. They set high standards for themselves, seek out challenging opportunities, and are motivated by the prospect of achieving significant milestones in their careers.

The role of ambition in career growth can be understood through various theoretical frameworks. One such framework is Abraham Maslow's hierarchy of needs, which posits that individuals are motivated by a series of hierarchical needs, culminating in self-actualization. In the context of career growth, ambition can be seen as a manifestation of the desire for self-actualization, where individuals strive to realize their potential, achieve mastery in their field, and make meaningful contributions. Ambition drives individuals to seek out opportunities for growth, pursue further education and training, and take on roles that align with their long-term career aspirations.

However, ambition alone is not sufficient for career growth; it must be supported by opportunities for development and advancement. Organizations play a crucial role in facilitating career growth by providing resources, training, and pathways for progression. Effective talent management strategies, such as mentorship programs, leadership development initiatives, and succession planning, can help individuals translate their ambitions into tangible career advancements. Organizations that foster a culture of continuous learning and development are better positioned to support their employees' career growth and retain top talent.

Career satisfaction, on the other hand, is a subjective experience that reflects an individual's overall contentment with their career. It encompasses various dimensions, including job satisfaction, work-life balance, alignment with personal values, and the sense of purpose and achievement derived from one's work. Career satisfaction is influenced by both intrinsic and extrinsic factors. Intrinsic factors relate to the inherent qualities of the work itself, such as the level of challenge, autonomy, and opportunities for creativity and innovation. Extrinsic factors include external rewards such as salary, benefits, recognition, and job security.

The relationship between ambition and career satisfaction is complex and can vary depending on individual circumstances and contexts. For some individuals, high levels of ambition may lead to significant career advancements and, consequently, higher levels of satisfaction. Achieving ambitious goals can provide a sense of accomplishment, boost self-esteem, and enhance overall career fulfillment. However, the pursuit of ambition can also come with challenges and trade-offs. For instance, highly ambitious individuals may experience increased stress, work-life imbalance, and pressure to constantly perform at high levels. If these challenges are not managed effectively, they can undermine career satisfaction and lead to burnout.

Balancing ambition with career satisfaction requires a nuanced understanding of one's goals, values, and priorities. It involves setting realistic and achievable goals, seeking out roles and opportunities that align with one's strengths and interests, and maintaining a healthy work-life balance. Self-awareness is key to this process, as it enables individuals to identify their intrinsic motivations, recognize their limits, and make informed decisions about their career paths. Additionally, cultivating resilience and adaptability can help individuals navigate the uncertainties and challenges of their career journey.

Professional development and lifelong learning are critical components of career growth. In a rapidly changing work environment characterized by technological advancements, globalization, and evolving industry trends, continuous learning is essential for staying relevant and competitive. Investing in education, training, and skill development can open up new career opportunities, enhance job performance, and increase career satisfaction. Organizations that support employee development through training programs, tuition assistance, and opportunities for skill enhancement contribute to a culture of growth and innovation.

Mentorship and networking are also important for career growth. Mentorship provides individuals with guidance, support, and insights from more experienced professionals, helping them navigate their career paths and overcome challenges. Effective mentorship relationships can foster professional growth, build confidence, and provide valuable opportunities for learning and development. Networking, on the other hand, involves building relationships with peers, colleagues, industry professionals, and potential employers. A strong professional network can provide access to job opportunities, industry knowledge, and collaborative partnerships, all of which can enhance career growth and satisfaction.

Work-life balance is a crucial factor in achieving career satisfaction. Balancing professional responsibilities with personal and family life is essential for maintaining overall well-being and avoiding burnout. Organizations that prioritize work-life balance through flexible work arrangements, supportive policies, and a culture of respect for personal time contribute to higher levels of employee satisfaction and retention. For individuals, setting boundaries, managing time effectively, and prioritizing self-care are important strategies for achieving a balanced and fulfilling career.

Another aspect of career growth is the alignment of one's work with personal values and a sense of purpose. When individuals feel that their work is meaningful and contributes to a greater good, they are more likely to experience career satisfaction. This alignment can be achieved by seeking out roles and organizations that reflect one's values, engaging in work that has a positive impact, and finding ways to integrate personal passions with professional responsibilities. A sense of purpose can provide motivation, enhance job satisfaction, and contribute to long-term career fulfillment.

In the contemporary workforce, the concept of career growth is evolving, with an increasing emphasis on flexibility, adaptability, and non-linear career paths. Traditional career trajectories, characterized by steady progression within a single organization, are giving way to more dynamic and diverse career experiences. Freelancing, gig work, portfolio careers, and remote work are becoming more common, offering individuals greater autonomy and opportunities to pursue multiple interests and career paths simultaneously. This shift requires individuals to be proactive in managing their careers, continuously updating their skills, and embracing new opportunities for growth and development.

The role of technology in career growth cannot be overlooked. Digital tools and platforms have transformed the way individuals learn, work, and connect with others. Online learning platforms, professional networking sites, and digital collaboration tools have expanded access to education, career resources, and job opportunities. Leveraging technology for career growth involves staying informed about industry trends, utilizing digital tools for skill development, and engaging with professional communities online.

Chapter 38: Community and Belonging: Finding My Tribe

Community and belonging are fundamental aspects of the human experience, deeply rooted in our evolutionary history and essential for our psychological well-being. The search for a sense of community and belonging—finding one's tribe—reflects the intrinsic human need for connection, acceptance, and identity. This journey involves exploring various social groups, cultures, and environments, and ultimately discovering where one feels most at home, understood, and valued. The concepts of community and belonging encompass a wide range of experiences, from familial bonds and friendships to professional networks and cultural affiliations.

From an evolutionary perspective, the need for community and belonging can be traced back to our early ancestors. For early humans, belonging to a group was crucial for survival. Living in communities provided protection from predators, increased access to resources, and opportunities for social learning and cooperation. This evolutionary legacy has shaped our social instincts and the importance we place on forming and maintaining social bonds. Even in modern society, where survival does not depend on group membership in the same way, the psychological need for belonging remains strong.

At its core, belonging is about feeling accepted and valued within a group. It involves being seen and understood, having one's contributions recognized, and sharing common values, goals, and experiences with others. The experience of belonging can provide a sense of identity, purpose, and emotional support, which are critical for overall well-being. Conversely, the absence of belonging—experiencing social isolation or exclusion—can have detrimental effects on mental health, including increased feelings of loneliness, anxiety, and depression.

The journey to finding one's tribe often begins in childhood, within the context of family and early social interactions. Family provides the first experience of belonging, where children learn social norms, values, and behaviors. Positive family relationships characterized by love, support, and open communication foster a strong sense of belonging and security. These early experiences shape individuals' expectations and behaviors in future social interactions and relationships.

As children grow, they begin to explore social connections beyond the family, forming friendships and participating in group activities such as school, sports, and hobbies. Friendships during childhood and adolescence are crucial for social development, providing opportunities to practice social skills, build empathy, and develop a sense of identity. Peer groups become important sources of belonging, offering a space where individuals can share experiences, interests, and support. The dynamics of peer relationships, including acceptance, rejection, and peer pressure, play a significant role in shaping one's sense of belonging and self-esteem.

The search for belonging continues into adulthood, where individuals navigate various social, professional, and cultural environments. In the workplace, finding a sense of community and belonging is essential for job satisfaction, engagement, and productivity. Workplace culture, team dynamics, and leadership practices influence employees' sense of belonging. Inclusive and supportive work environments that value diversity, encourage collaboration, and recognize individual contributions foster a strong sense of community. Professional networks and mentorship relationships also contribute to a sense of belonging, providing opportunities for growth, support, and connection within one's career field.

Cultural and community affiliations further shape the experience of belonging. Cultural identity, encompassing ethnicity, nationality, religion, and traditions, provides a sense of continuity, shared history, and collective values. Engaging with cultural communities, participating in cultural practices, and connecting with others who share similar backgrounds can strengthen cultural identity and belonging. Community organizations, social clubs, and interest-based groups offer additional avenues for finding one's tribe, where individuals can connect over shared passions, causes, and activities.

The digital age has transformed the way people seek and experience belonging. Social media, online forums, and virtual communities provide new platforms for connection, allowing individuals to find and engage with like-minded people across geographical boundaries. These digital spaces can offer support, information, and a sense of belonging, particularly for those who may feel isolated or marginalized in their offline environments. However, the digital realm also presents challenges, such as the potential for superficial connections, online harassment, and the impact of social comparison on self-esteem.

The psychological benefits of belonging are well-documented. A strong sense of belonging is associated with higher levels of happiness, life satisfaction, and mental health. It enhances resilience, helping individuals cope with stress and adversity by providing social support and a sense of stability. Belonging also fosters a sense of purpose and motivation, as individuals are more likely to engage in activities and pursue goals that are valued by their community.

Conversely, the lack of belonging can have serious negative effects. Social isolation and loneliness are linked to a range of mental health issues, including depression, anxiety, and substance abuse. Chronic loneliness can also have physical health implications, such as increased risk of cardiovascular disease and weakened immune function. The experience of exclusion or marginalization can lead to feelings of worthlessness, low self-esteem, and a sense of alienation.

Belonging is not static; it evolves over time as individuals move through different life stages, roles, and environments. Major life transitions, such as moving to a new city, starting a new job, or experiencing a loss, can disrupt one's sense of belonging and necessitate the search for new connections and communities. Navigating these transitions requires adaptability, openness to new experiences, and proactive efforts to build and maintain social connections.

The concept of belonging also intersects with issues of diversity, inclusion, and social justice. For many individuals, finding a sense of belonging involves navigating systems of privilege and oppression that shape access to social, economic, and cultural resources. Marginalized groups, including people of color, LGBTQ+ individuals, immigrants, and people with disabilities, may face additional barriers to belonging due to discrimination, prejudice, and systemic inequities. Efforts to create inclusive communities and promote social justice are essential for ensuring that all individuals have the opportunity to find and experience belonging.

Inclusive practices, such as promoting diversity, fostering open dialogue, and challenging biases, contribute to creating environments where everyone can feel valued and accepted. Building inclusive communities involves recognizing and addressing power dynamics, providing equitable access to resources and opportunities, and creating spaces where diverse perspectives and experiences are respected and celebrated.

In educational settings, fostering a sense of belonging is crucial for student engagement, academic success, and overall well-being. Schools and universities can promote belonging by creating supportive and inclusive learning environments, offering programs and services that address students' diverse needs, and encouraging participation in extracurricular activities and student organizations. Positive relationships with peers, teachers, and mentors play a key role in students' sense of belonging and their ability to thrive academically and personally.

The role of leadership in fostering belonging cannot be overstated. Leaders in various contexts, from families and schools to workplaces and communities, have the power to shape the culture and dynamics of their groups. Effective leaders promote belonging by modeling inclusive behaviors, building trust, recognizing individual contributions, and creating opportunities for meaningful engagement and collaboration. Leadership that prioritizes empathy, respect, and equity can inspire and empower individuals to connect and contribute to their communities.

Chapter 39: Self-Reflection: Understanding My Journey

Self-reflection is a profound and transformative process that involves introspection and analysis of one's thoughts, feelings, behaviors, and experiences. It is the act of looking inward to gain a deeper understanding of oneself, one's journey through life, and the factors that shape one's identity and actions. Engaging in self-reflection allows individuals to gain insights into their values, beliefs, motivations, strengths, and areas for growth, thereby fostering personal development and emotional well-being. This process is crucial for developing self-awareness, making informed decisions, and cultivating a fulfilling and meaningful life.

The journey of self-reflection begins with the recognition of the need to pause and examine one's life. In the hustle and bustle of daily activities, it is easy to become caught up in routines and external demands, often neglecting the internal world. Self-reflection provides an opportunity to step back, detach from immediate concerns, and take a holistic view of one's experiences and inner landscape. This initial step requires intentionality and a willingness to engage in honest and sometimes uncomfortable self-examination.

One of the fundamental aspects of self-reflection is the exploration of past experiences. By revisiting significant events, both positive and negative, individuals can uncover patterns and themes that have influenced their development. Reflecting on childhood experiences, relationships, educational and career milestones, and pivotal life events can reveal how these moments have shaped one's beliefs, attitudes, and behaviors. Understanding the impact of past experiences provides valuable context for current actions and decisions, allowing individuals to address unresolved issues and heal from past wounds.

Self-reflection also involves examining one's values and beliefs. Values are the principles and standards that guide one's behavior and decision-making, while beliefs are the convictions and assumptions that shape one's worldview. Reflecting on these core aspects helps individuals identify what truly matters to them and whether their actions align with their values and beliefs. This process can lead to greater authenticity and integrity, as individuals strive to live in accordance with their deepest convictions.

Another crucial component of self-reflection is the assessment of one's strengths and areas for growth. Identifying and acknowledging strengths fosters self-confidence and provides a foundation for leveraging these attributes in various aspects of life. Simultaneously, recognizing areas for growth encourages a mindset of continuous improvement and learning. Self-reflection enables individuals to set realistic goals and develop strategies for personal and professional development, ultimately enhancing their overall effectiveness and satisfaction.

Emotional self-reflection involves exploring one's feelings and emotional responses to different situations. Emotions are powerful indicators of underlying thoughts and beliefs, and understanding them can provide insights into one's motivations and triggers. Reflecting on emotions allows individuals to develop emotional intelligence, which includes the ability to recognize, understand, and manage one's emotions, as well as the capacity to empathize with others. Emotional self-reflection promotes emotional regulation, resilience, and healthier interpersonal relationships.

The practice of self-reflection can take various forms, each offering unique benefits and approaches. Journaling is a common and effective method, allowing individuals to document their thoughts, feelings, and experiences in writing. The act of writing helps clarify and organize thoughts, making it easier to identify patterns and gain insights.

Regular journaling creates a record of one's journey, providing a tangible reference for tracking progress and growth over time.

Meditation and mindfulness practices are also powerful tools for self-reflection. These practices involve cultivating present-moment awareness and non-judgmental observation of one's thoughts and feelings. Meditation creates a space for introspection, allowing individuals to observe their internal experiences without attachment or distraction. Mindfulness practices enhance self-awareness, reduce stress, and promote a deeper connection with oneself.

Engaging in reflective conversations with trusted friends, mentors, or therapists can further enrich the self-reflection process. These interactions provide external perspectives and feedback, helping individuals see aspects of themselves that they might overlook. Constructive feedback and supportive dialogue can challenge existing assumptions and encourage new ways of thinking, fostering personal growth and self-discovery.

Artistic expression, such as drawing, painting, music, or creative writing, offers another avenue for self-reflection. Creative activities provide a means to explore and express emotions and experiences that might be difficult to articulate verbally. Artistic expression can reveal subconscious thoughts and feelings, offering a deeper understanding of one's inner world. Engaging in creative processes also promotes relaxation, stress relief, and a sense of accomplishment.

The benefits of self-reflection extend beyond personal development to impact various aspects of life, including relationships, career, and overall well-being. In relationships, self-reflection enhances communication and empathy by fostering a better understanding of one's needs, boundaries, and emotional responses. It enables individuals to identify and address patterns of behavior that may contribute to conflicts or misunderstandings, leading to healthier and more fulfilling connections.

In the context of career and professional development, self-reflection supports goal setting, decision-making, and performance improvement. By assessing one's strengths, values, and interests, individuals can make informed career choices that align with their passions and aspirations. Reflecting on past achievements and challenges provides insights into areas for skill development and professional growth. Self-reflection also promotes a proactive approach to career planning, encouraging individuals to seek opportunities for advancement and adapt to changing circumstances.

Overall well-being is significantly influenced by the practice of self-reflection. It fosters a sense of purpose and direction, helping individuals align their actions with their values and goals. Self-reflection reduces stress and enhances emotional regulation by providing a space to process and understand one's experiences. It cultivates resilience by encouraging a growth mindset and the ability to learn from setbacks. Ultimately, self-reflection contributes to a greater sense of fulfillment, meaning, and satisfaction in life.

Despite its many benefits, self-reflection can be challenging and requires a commitment to introspection and self-honesty. It involves confronting uncomfortable truths, acknowledging mistakes, and taking responsibility for one's actions. Resistance to self-reflection may arise from fear of facing negative emotions or fear of change. However, embracing these challenges is essential for genuine growth and transformation. Developing a regular practice of self-reflection, even in small increments, can lead to significant and lasting benefits.

Incorporating self-reflection into daily life involves creating intentional moments for introspection. This can be as simple as setting aside a few minutes each day to reflect on one's thoughts and feelings or as structured as scheduling regular reflection sessions. Finding a quiet and comfortable space, free from distractions, can enhance the quality of self-reflection. Combining self-reflection with other self-care practices, such as exercise, relaxation, and healthy living, supports overall well-being and balance.

As individuals navigate the complexities of modern life, the ability to engage in self-reflection becomes increasingly valuable. It serves as a compass, guiding individuals through personal and professional challenges and helping them stay true to their values and aspirations. By understanding their journey, individuals can make more intentional choices, cultivate meaningful relationships, and create a life that reflects their true selves.

Chapter 40: The Whole Picture: Embracing Who I Am

Embracing who you are—understanding and accepting the whole picture of your identity, strengths, weaknesses, experiences, and values—is a profound and transformative journey. This process involves recognizing and honoring all aspects of yourself, from the traits that you take pride in to those you may struggle with, and from your past experiences to your future aspirations. It is a holistic approach to self-acceptance that requires introspection, self-compassion, and a willingness to confront and integrate all parts of your being.

The journey of embracing who you are begins with self-awareness. Self-awareness is the foundation of understanding your unique identity, which encompasses your personality traits, emotional responses, motivations, and values. Developing self-awareness involves paying close attention to your thoughts, feelings, and behaviors in various situations. It requires honest reflection and a non-judgmental attitude towards yourself. Tools such as journaling, mindfulness practices, and feedback from trusted individuals can facilitate this process by providing insights into your patterns and tendencies.

Recognizing and appreciating your strengths is an important aspect of embracing who you are. Your strengths are the qualities, skills, and abilities that you naturally excel in or have developed over time. Identifying your strengths involves reflecting on your accomplishments, acknowledging the positive feedback you receive from others, and recognizing the activities that bring you joy and fulfillment. Embracing your strengths allows you to build confidence, leverage your talents in meaningful ways, and contribute positively to your personal and professional life.

Equally important is acknowledging your weaknesses and areas for growth. Everyone has aspects of themselves that they may view as limitations or challenges. These could include certain personality traits, habits, or skills that you find difficult to manage or improve. Embracing your weaknesses does not mean resigning yourself to them but rather accepting them as part of your whole self. It involves understanding the impact of these weaknesses on your life, being compassionate towards yourself, and taking proactive steps to address or manage them. This process fosters resilience and a growth mindset, encouraging continuous learning and self-improvement.

Another critical component of embracing who you are is understanding your values and beliefs. Values are the principles and standards that guide your behavior and decision-making. They are deeply influenced by your upbringing, culture, and personal experiences. Reflecting on your values involves identifying what matters most to you, what you stand for, and how you want to live your life. Understanding your values helps you make decisions that are aligned with your true self, leading to greater authenticity and fulfillment.

Your beliefs, on the other hand, are the convictions and assumptions you hold about yourself, others, and the world. Some beliefs are empowering and motivate you to pursue your goals, while others may be limiting and hold you back. Embracing who you are involves examining your beliefs, challenging those that are unhelpful or outdated, and reinforcing those that support your well-being and growth. This process requires introspection, critical thinking, and sometimes the courage to change long-held perspectives.

Past experiences play a significant role in shaping your identity and sense of self. Reflecting on your past can provide valuable insights into your current behaviors, attitudes, and emotional responses. This includes acknowledging both positive and negative experiences, understanding how they have influenced you, and recognizing the lessons learned from them. Embracing your past involves accepting it as an integral part of your journey without allowing it to define you entirely. It is about finding meaning in your experiences and using that understanding to inform your present and future actions.

Emotional self-awareness is another essential element of embracing who you are. Emotions are powerful indicators of your inner state and can provide valuable information about your needs, desires, and boundaries. Developing emotional self-awareness involves recognizing and understanding your emotional responses, identifying the triggers that elicit certain emotions, and learning to express and manage your emotions healthily. Embracing your emotions means accepting them as valid and important aspects of your experience, rather than suppressing or denying them.

The process of embracing who you are also involves cultivating self-compassion. Self-compassion is the practice of treating yourself with kindness, understanding, and forgiveness, especially in moments of difficulty or failure. It involves recognizing that imperfection is part of the human experience and that everyone makes mistakes and faces challenges. Practicing self-compassion helps you build resilience, reduce self-criticism, and foster a more positive and supportive relationship with yourself.

Relationships with others play a significant role in the journey of self-acceptance. Interactions with family, friends, colleagues, and romantic partners can influence how you see yourself and how you feel about your identity. Healthy, supportive relationships provide a sense of belonging and validation, helping you embrace who you are. Conversely, toxic or unsupportive relationships can undermine your self-esteem and sense of self-worth. It is important to surround yourself with people who accept and appreciate you for who you are, and to set boundaries with those who do not.

Cultural and societal influences also impact your self-perception and acceptance. Societal norms, cultural expectations, and media representations can shape your beliefs about what is desirable or acceptable. These external influences can create pressure to conform to certain standards or ideals, often leading to self-doubt and dissatisfaction. Embracing who you are involves critically examining these influences, recognizing their impact, and choosing to prioritize your own values and authenticity over external validation.

Personal growth and self-acceptance are ongoing processes that evolve over time. As you move through different stages of life, your experiences, priorities, and perspectives may change. Embracing who you are means being open to this evolution and allowing yourself to grow and adapt. It involves being patient and compassionate with yourself as you navigate new challenges and opportunities.

In addition to introspection and self-awareness, embracing who you are involves taking action to live in alignment with your true self. This includes setting and pursuing goals that reflect your values and aspirations, making decisions that honor your needs and boundaries, and engaging in activities that bring you joy and fulfillment. It also means advocating for yourself, seeking support when needed, and being willing to make changes that enhance your well-being and authenticity.

The benefits of embracing "who you are" are profound and far-reaching. When you accept and honor all aspects of yourself, you experience greater self-confidence, emotional stability, and overall well-being. You are more likely to build meaningful and authentic relationships, pursue fulfilling goals, and navigate life's challenges with resilience and grace. Embracing who you are allows you to live a life that is true to your values and aspirations, fostering a deep sense of purpose and satisfaction.

Epilogue

As the final pieces of our puzzle fall into place, we stand back and marvel at the intricate tapestry of our lives. "The Puzzle of Me: Discovering the Why Behind Me" has taken us on a profound journey through the myriad experiences that shape our identities, revealing the delicate interplay of moments and choices that define us.

Looking back, we see how the foundation laid in our earliest years set the stage for our growth. The love and guidance of our families, the friendships that offered companionship and challenge, and the educational milestones that sparked our curiosity—each contributed to the formation of our self-concept. These early experiences were the cornerstones upon which we built our understanding of the world and our place within it.

Adolescence, with its turbulence and transformation, brought us face to face with the quest for identity. The struggles and triumphs of these years tested our resilience and shaped our values. Through the lens of first love, academic pressures, and social dynamics, we learned to navigate the complexities of our emotions and relationships. These formative years were a crucible, forging the raw material of our character into something more refined and resilient.

As we ventured into adulthood, the lessons of our youth were put to the test. The pursuit of independence, the challenges of career and relationships, and the quest for personal fulfillment required us to draw on the strengths we had developed. We faced setbacks and celebrated successes, each adding depth to our understanding of ourselves. The responsibilities and freedoms of adulthood demanded that we balance ambition with self-care, striving for growth while maintaining our well-being.

Throughout this journey, we encountered moments of profound introspection. We confronted our fears, celebrated our achievements, and mourned our losses. Each chapter of our lives, each piece of our puzzle, added complexity and richness to our self-portrait. In reflecting on these experiences, we gained clarity about the forces that have shaped us and the unique mosaic that we have become.

Now, as we close this book, we carry forward the wisdom and insights we have gained. The journey of self-discovery is never truly complete; it is an ongoing process of learning, growing, and evolving. We continue to encounter new challenges and opportunities, each offering a chance to add another piece to our puzzle.

Remember that the "why" behind you is a dynamic and ever-changing story. Embrace the journey with curiosity and compassion, knowing that each experience, whether joyful or painful, contributes to the richness of your life. Celebrate your uniqueness, honor your journey, and continue to explore the depths of who you are.

Thank you for joining me on this exploration of self-discovery. May you find inspiration and empowerment in the intricate puzzle of your own life, and may you continue to discover and appreciate the profound beauty of being you.

The End.